CHAUCER MEMORIAL LECTURES,

1900.

READ BEFORE THE ROYAL SOCIETY OF
LITERATURE.

EDITED, WITH AN INTRODUCTION,

BY

PERCY W. AMES, F.S.A.,

SECRETARY R.S.L.

LONDON:
ASHER AND CO.,
13, BEDFORD STREET, W.C
1900.

PRINTED BY ADLARD AND SON,
BARTHOLOMEW CLOSE, E.C.

PREFACE.

———

THIS volume is the result of a proposal made by Dr. Phené that the Royal Society of Literature should commemorate the Quingentenary of the death of Chaucer, who died in the year 1400, by some such memorial of the poet as should be distinctively associated with the Society.

As no opportunity for the publication of inedited MSS. relating to Chaucer, or of original work concerning his poems, appeared likely to arise, a course of popular lectures on his Life, Times, and Works, as they appear in the new light of modern criticism, was decided upon as the most appropriate method of giving effect to the suggestion.

CONTENTS.

INTRODUCTION.

In the decline of the year 1400 Geoffrey Chaucer, in apparently a premature old age, sank to his rest with the closing century, to submit like it to the judgment and verdict of posterity. The study of history, it has been well said, is a "discipline in candour, toleration, and impartiality of judgment;" and when we sum up the fourteenth century we may pass over the brutality of the penal code, and remember instead that the period saw completed the amalgamation of antagonistic races and the formation of the modern English people; the triumph of the English tongue; the abolition of English serfdom; the development and consolidation of the English Constitution. The nineteenth century is likewise passing away, to be criticised, admired, scorned, pitied, and perhaps ridiculed by our most superior and accomplished descendants. As it recedes further into the past, and the future historian obtains a comprehensive understanding of its anomalies impossible to us who are near it and of it, and records its successes and its failures, its glories and its mistakes, he will not omit, it is to be hoped, to observe among its inconspicuous and less imposing features an amiable and praiseworthy virtue, its almost exclusive possession. This is manifested in the desire to possess and the earnest effort to obtain precise and accurate knowledge of our illustrious predecessors; to do justice to their talents and merits, and in the case of real genius to endeavour to rekindle its vitalising and stimulating power; to arouse popular interest, sympathy, and gratitude towards the thought and work of the past.

The perennial freshness of so bright, pellucid, and lively a writer as Chaucer might be considered to possess an attraction sufficient in itself to dispense with the need of any advertisement, especially as it is open and available to all; but if the unceasing beauty of the sky remained unregarded by many until John Ruskin opened their eyes, the accessibility of a delightful poet presents no sort of argument against the necessity for such aids as these. A more particular criticism might be based upon the supposed superfluity of further attempts of the sort. In view of the immense quantity of really valuable matter already published by such writers as Tyrwhitt,* Nicholas,† Professor Ten Brink, the distinguished Dutch philologist,‡ Warton,§ Lowell,|| Dr. Furnivall,¶ and Professors Skeat,** Child,†† Hales,‡‡ and Ward,§§ it may be asked, what justification is there for these lectures, especially in the absence of any claim of new discovery or fresh

* Introductory Discourse to the 'Canterbury Tales.'
† 'Life of Chaucer.'
‡ 'Chaucer-Studien.'
§ 'History of English Poetry.'
|| 'My Study Windows.'
¶ Six-text edition of the 'Canterbury Tales.'
** 'The Complete Works of Geoffrey Chaucer,' and numerous other publications.
†† 'Observations on the Language of Chaucer and Gower.'
‡‡ 'Chambers' Encyclopædia.'
§§ "Chaucer" ('English Men of Letters').

criticism? An answer to such pertinent inquiry in respect of general literature is given in a defence of literary lectures contained in my Address on the Study of English Literature introductory to our last course of afternoon lectures,* and need not be repeated. With regard to the study of Chaucer it must be remembered that between those giants of energetic research, commentary, and criticism, and the general reader there seems to be a gulf fixed, which by no means implies the absence of literary charm and attractiveness in the form in which their noble efforts are put forth, but indicates probably a mistaken impression that much mental effort is needed for their perusal; at all events, with the exception of a comparatively small number of enterprising and adventurous readers, this vast field of research continues practically unknown, and the delight of first-hand acquaintance with Chaucer unfelt. The function of the middle man in scientific study was long ago pointed out. One of the very few suggestions of Auguste Comte with which Mr. Herbert Spencer found himself in entire accord was the proposed formation of a new order of scientific men, whose function should be that of co-ordinating the results arrived at by the rest. The literary specialists may be indebted similarly to the lectures of their immediate students, in order that the actual monuments of genius, separated from inferior productions ignorantly included with them in an uncritical age, and freed from textual and other errors that have crept in during the course of time, may be brought to the homes of the people,

* 'Afternoon Lectures on English Literature,' London, 1893

and take their proper place " among those influences by which nations are at once moulded and refined and elevated."

No doubt sometimes (and we say it with no want of respect to the authority of the commentators, or undervaluation of their discoveries) we are tempted to wish they would take a well-earned holiday and leave us alone with our favourites, when even if we make mistakes we can at least yield to our natural inclinations and indulge in unaffected enjoyment; for after all it will not be disputed that Chaucer and Shakespeare are more delightful company than even the most learned and industrious of their commentators. We may further venture to assert that by abandoning ourselves to the enjoyment of that ever-fresh and vital literature, and reading critical documents but sparingly, our taste and judgment will be at once more delicate and sure than by spending much time in the literary dissecting room. As Sainte-Beuve has said with reference to the present fashion of research, that if it is allowed to prevail, if curiosity wins the day over art, "people would come on the whole to prefer the materials to the work, the scaffolding to the monument." Much of the product of research, moreover, seems to belong to history quite as much as to literature. We do not wish to criticise the critics, nor do we wish to imply by this modest memorial anything beyond the fact that we realise our indebtedness to Chaucer as one of the few writers of the past whose works we can still read for the pleasure they afford us. If we do not pretend to the critical spirit at its highest pitch of intelligence,

we can at least invite our hearers and readers to a
consideration of our own studies; to our interpre-
tation and rendering of more learned commentators;
to a share in our own enjoyment, in the hope of
awakening some degree of appreciative sympathy.
The more we learn, from the statistics of libraries
and other sources of information, of the tastes of
the general reader, the more clear becomes the
necessity for such aids as are afforded by the
popular lecture. Coleridge, developing an idea
derived from the Mishna, divided readers into
four classes. The first he compared to an hour-
glass; their reading being as the sand—it runs in
and runs out, and leaves not a vestige behind. A
second class, he said, resembled a sponge, which
imbibes everything and returns it in nearly the
same state, only a little dirtier. A third class he
likened to a jelly-bag, which allows all that is pure
to pass away, and retains only the refuse and the
dregs. The fourth class he compared to the
slaves in the diamond mines of Golconda, who,
casting aside all that is worthless, preserved only
the pure gem. Notwithstanding the high authority
of *Dogberry*, reading does not always come by
nature; it owes much to direction and guidance,
especially when it comprises the study of what we
agree to call *genius*. We cannot discover the
source of genius by observing its circumstances,
its opportunities, its experiences, its contact with
other minds, access to books, foreign travel, etc.,—
these supply but the material, or at most a method;
nor can we discover it in any of the ordinary aims
and ambitions that lend so much movement and

interest to the drama of human life. On this quest we must search deep in the human spirit before we find the originating and impelling force, far more intense than these, a pure passion that glows with the kindling of intellectual fire; an inextinguishable flame, fed by visions of ideal beauty which penetrate the soul. The function of the critic, that is of the nobler sort who take to their work "because they have a natural gift that way, and not simply because they have failed in literature," is something higher and more important than merely to detect faults and weaknesses and hold them up to ridicule. He should, indeed, be always wakeful and on the alert, but chiefly to discover new talent, not to "wreck budding reputations." The well-informed critic has splendid opportunities in the ordinary practice of his profession of preserving a standard of beauty, and of encouraging the art which elevates and never degrades. Poetry, the crowned queen of the arts, attracts us by many qualities; its music, the affluence of its imagery, the exquisite choice of words and the harmony and felicity of their arrangement; but beyond, above, and beneath all these sources of sensuous delight there exists something that excites further emotions; something that baffles description, that is wholly supersensuous and spiritual, which wafts us airs from the immortal regions, and gives us brief glimpses of the deeper significance of life. The history of English poetry tells us of wonderful poetic ages when the divine fire kindled many hearts at once; also of times when the "loved of the gods" dwelt in comparative isolation in the midst of an unpoetic generation, unsustained by the sweet consolations of poetic association or the tender endearments of poetic sympathy, such as Milton, whose "soul was like a star and dwelt apart." In some degree Chaucer may be said to have stood alone. By far the most gifted writer of his age, he was the only humorist, and probably a more devoted book-lover than any of his contemporaries, and much of his mental life must have been solitary; on the other hand, his frank geniality, his manliness, the simplicity and directness of his style, the abundant evidence of his wide, shrewd, and accurate observation, all seem to indicate that he enjoyed and lived fully the life of his time. In the *Athenæum* of June 17th, 1899, there is a short but interesting notice of poems by S. Mallarmé and W. B. Yeats, in the course of which the reviewer says, "There are poets, then, who accept this normal life, whose vitality responds to the stimulus of its claims, and who find no higher task for their art than that of heightening and glorifying its flow with imaginative magic;" and taking Mr. Rudyard Kipling for illustration, he says further, "Himself a transfigured man in the street, he naturally speaks in accents which the man in the street recognises." Here we have neatly put a passage which admirably applies to Chaucer. If the man in the street, that is the ordinary busy man of affairs, would only take the trouble, reduced to a minimum by Prof. Skeat's assistance, to overcome the trifling difficulties presented by Chaucer's archaisms and "indifferent spelling," and read the whole of his works, not

only would he find himself in contact with a
thoroughly healthy and practical mind, but such a
study would add to the store of life's pleasures,
and most agreeably convey much real and interesting knowledge of the English tongue ; and, as from
the study of any great poet, a wider literary horizon
is perceived thereafter by the inevitable raising of
the standard of taste. The mastery of Chaucer
makes it possible and agreeable to study " moral
Gower" and other early writers. The literary
contemporaries of Chaucer have furnished material
for one of these lectures in which many points of
interest are brought out. The latter half of the
fourteenth century, deeply interesting for its social,
economic, and intellectual progress, is also remarkable for its literary activity. That industrious
inventor and collector of 'Travellers' Tales,' Sir
John Mandeville, produced his entertaining work
in 1356, when Chaucer was about sixteen years
of age. He is said to have maintained that the
earth was round, a valiant contention at that
time ; but as he had also discovered Adam's apple
tree, " the fruit of which has a bite out of one
side," his geographical theory was not taken as
seriously as it deserved. With increased knowledge
of the countries described by Sir John, and succes-
sive discoveries of earlier books of travel, whence
he evidently derived most of his materials, his fame
as an explorer and original observer has steadily
diminished, so that his literary faculty is almost all
that is left to him. Unfortunately, however, for
the reputation he has so long enjoyed of being the
father of English prose, it is now regarded as certain

that he wrote in Latin and in French only, the English version being a translation made a century later. Wiclif, too, although chiefly remembered either as the morning star of the Reformation or as the cross of the conservative High Church party, deserves mention for his literary gift. He certainly displays a quality of simplicity in his translation of the Bible which at once captivates the reader ; it possesses an attractive spell which modern scholarship cannot be said to have cast over the Revised Version, *e. g.*—

"And a womman that hadde suffride many thingis of ful many lechis, and spendid alle hir thingis, and no-thing prophitide, but more hadde worse, whanne she hadde herd of Jhesu, she cam in the cumpanye byhynde, and touchide his cloth."

Of all Chaucer's literary contemporaries, it is perhaps Langland who exhibits his most complete contrast. These two men supply a most interesting illustration of how a difference in individual temperament makes the colours of the pageant of life appear brilliant or sad. Mr. Francis Turner Palgrave has expressed this idea so effectively that I venture to quote his fine lines describing the contrasted attitudes of the two poets. Chaucer's work was, he says,

" To paint
With Nature's freshness, what before him lies ;
The knave, the fool, the frolicsome, the quaint ;
His the broad jest, the laugh without restraint,
The ready tears, the spirit lightly moved ;
Loving the world, and by the world beloved.
So forth fared Chaucer on his pilgrimage
Through England's humours ; in immortal song

Bodying the form and pressure of his age,
Tints gay as pure, and delicate as strong ;
Still to the Tabard the blythe travellers throng,
Seen in his mind so vividly, that we
Know them more clearly than the men we see.
O Poet of romance and courtly glee,
And downcast eager glance that shuns the sky,
Above, about, are signs thou canst not see ;
Portents in heaven and earth ! And one goes by
With other than thy prosperous, laughing eye,
Framing the rough web of his rueful lays,
The sorrow and the sin ; with bitter gaze,
As down the Strand he stalks, a sable shade
Of death, while, jingling like the elfin train,
In silver samite knight and dame and maid
Ride to the tourney on the barrier'd plain ;
And he must bow in humble mute disdain,
And that worst foe of baffled souls endure,
To see the evil that they may not cure."

Of another contemporary we know unfortunately
absolutely nothing beyond what his works contain,
and yet these reveal so much originality, as well as
refinement and elevation of tone, that it is as sur-
prising as regrettable that no information is to be
had about him, not even his name. Accepting the
view of Ten Brink as to date and unity of authorship, we must conclude that when Chaucer was
about twenty years of age the following interesting works appeared from the pen of the gifted
unknown :—' Morte Arthur,' ' Sir Gawayne and
the Green Knight,' ' The Pearl,' ' Clannesse,' and
' Patience.'

Chaucer was so great that it is not sufficient to
compare him only with his English contemporaries, and it is a gratification and pride to an

English student to remember that Chaucer has been bracketed with Dante and Petrarch in what has been called "the Triumvirate of the Mediæval Poets." Few things are more interesting in the literary life of Chaucer than those facts and ingenious guesses which seem to explain the source of the unmistakable Italian influence in his later writings, which show that the art and higher thought of Italy had penetrated his mind. It is worth noting that while French literature, language, and mode of thought exerted a general influence upon Chaucer from his earliest years, the influence of the Italian renaissance began at a definite period associated with his epoch-making journey to Genoa in 1372. Professor Ward says, "While neither the 'Romaunt of the Rose' (Chaucer's translation from the French) nor the 'Book of the Duchess' exhibits any traces of Italian influence, the same assertion cannot safely be made with regard to any important poem produced after the date of this Italian journey." The indications of this influence are to be found in direct allusions to Italian writers and their works; passages, plots, incidents, and ideas are borrowed and incorporated, and of these Mr. Axon gives in his lecture many illustrations. There was also a deeper influence shown chiefly in improved art. From this Italianization, as Mr. Palgrave remarks, Chaucer derived a "variety of range, a heightening of style, an improvement in poetic form, and these things liberated and gave full play to his splendid natural gifts." Careful and candid comparison of Chaucer with the famous three shows his affinity with Boccaccio rather than with the purer and loftier spirits of Dante and Petrarch, notwithstanding the fact that he was most affected by Dante. Chaucer resembled Boccaccio in an occasional levity, a bantering anticlericalism, a constant sense of humour, and an exuberant delight in mere existence. Great as the Italian influence was, and much as Chaucer's style and method reveal of his indebtedness, it has never been shown or allowed by any first-hand student of his works that he was a sort of English edition of Italian poetry. Although this influence varied during the last twenty-seven years of his life, sometimes more and sometimes less, it at no time obscured or even modified the essential quality of his mind.

Readers who have made their first acquaintance with Chaucer by the ' Milleres Tale ' are naturally repelled by the coarseness of its broad humour, and may thereafter deny themselves the profit and delight of a fuller and truer knowledge of the poet. Chaucer, like all other men worth studying, who lived in a moral and social atmosphere very different from our own, has a claim to sound and generous judgment.

One of the most useful aids to the study of Chaucer is to be found in the grouping of his works into three periods by Ten Brink. During the first of these periods, from his earliest writing to 1372, he copied the French, and exhibited that influence chiefly in ' The Romaunt of the Rose.' It was during this time that he also wrote the charming ' Book of the Duchess,' which, though somewhat crude, has many beauties and is full of promise; also the 'Second Nonnes Tale,' and parts of the 'Monkes Tale,' afterwards incorporated in the 'Canterbury Tales.' In the second period, 1373 to 1384, Chaucer derived his chief impulse from the Italian Renaissance, more particularly from the 'Divine Comedy' and Boccaccio's poems 'Il Teseide' and 'Il Filostrato.' It was during this time that he wrote 'The Clerkes Tale,' 'Palamon and Arcite,' 'Compleint to his Lady,' 'Compleint unto Pite,' 'The Personnes Tale,' 'Man of Lawes Tale,' 'Compleint of Mars,' 'Troilus and Criseyde,' 'Parlement of Foules,' and 'Hous of Fame.' In the third period, 1384 to 1400, are most clearly manifested the individuality and originality of Chaucer's genius, when his brilliant powers found full and free expression. To this period belong the 'Legend of Good Women,' several of the 'Canterbury Tales,' the 'Treatise on the Astrolabe,' 'Compleint of Venus,' 'Lenvoy to Scogan,' and 'Lenvoy to Bukton.' With regard to these last, it may be of interest to note that Henry Scogan is believed to have been a prosperous courtier and poet to whom Chaucer appealed for his recommendation to royal favour and help.

> "Scogan, that knelest at the stremes heed
>   Of grace, of alle honour and worthinesse,
>   In th'ende of which streme I am dul as deed,
>   Forgete in solitarie wildernesse,
>   Minne thy frend, ther it may fructifye!
>   Far-wel, and lok thou never eft Love defye!"

Of "maister Bukton" we know next to nothing, but in the 'Counseil of Chaucer touching Mariage,' which was sent to Bukton, we obtain plain indications, confirming several allusions to the same effect elsewhere, that Chaucer's married life was anything but blissful.

In contrast with the modern practice (developed to a ludicrous extent during the concluding quarter of the present century) of discovering and recording every minute detail concerning the habits, tastes, and opinions of living writers, little or nothing was related by admiring biographers of the authors of the past. Much that we should have liked to know, much that would have explained what is obscure, that would perhaps have added significance, beauty, interest, pathos, to passages in their works, is hidden from us. Efforts have vainly been made to detect the political and theological opinions of Chaucer, but it is as futile to seek for the special religious badge with which to label him, as it has always proved in the case of Shakespeare. The opening lines to the prologue to the ' Legend of Good Women' indicate plainly enough that Chaucer distinguished between knowledge derived from tradition and taught by authority, and knowledge capable of verification.

" A thousand tymés have I herd men telle,
That ther is joye in heven, and peyne in helle ;
And I acordé wel that hit is so ;
But nathélés, yit wot I wel also,
That ther his noon dwellíng in this contrée,
That either hath in heven or helle y-be,
Ne may of hit non other weyes witén,
But as he hath herd seyd, or foundé hit writén ;
For by assay ther may no man hit preve."

The study of the sources of the 'Canterbury Tales' reveals the extensive reading of Chaucer, and at the same time the unblushing plagiarism of early writers. Chaucer and Shakespeare, though of course in different degrees of excellence and vivifying power, so frequently make dry bones live; transform dull chronicles, legends, and stupid tales into literary gems, sparkling with animation and the true realism, and invested with the deepest interest, that we are apt to think that *all* their borrowings are of the same nature, whereas in both cases much admired scenes, episodes, phrases, and entire passages are incorporated from other sources than the brain of the poet. It is doubtful if there is a single indication in Shakespeare that he ever gave a thought to the matter. That mysterious being was as insensible to any supposed rights of other authors as he was indifferent to his own; the offspring of genius, both thought and expression, were apparently assumed to be common property. Chaucer, on the other hand, seemed to be conscious of this wholesale borrowing, and occasionally tried to mislead and mystify his readers. Of 'Troilus and Criseyde,' his greatest completed work, one third was borrowed from the 'Filostrato' of Boccaccio, but instead of acknowledging or ignoring the fact, he professes to be translating out of Latin from an author named Lollius ! The 'Phisiciens Tale' was taken from ' Le Roman de la Rose,' but Chaucer omits to mention the circumstance, and instead he copies the obligation of the French author to Livy, making it appear that he had it direct from the Latin, " Ther was, as telleth Titus Livius," &c. It would be entirely wrong to conclude from this habit that Chaucer was inclined to make large claims for himself, and to over-estimate his gifts and powers. On the contrary, as Professor Ward has observed, "one very pleasing quality in Chaucer must have been his modesty; . . . . again and again he disclaims all boasts of perfection, or pretensions to pre-eminence, as a poet." To quote again from the prologue to the 'Legend of Good Women,' he says:

> "Allas! that I ne had English, ryme or prose,
> Suffisant this flour to preyse aright!
> But helpeth, ye that han conning and might,
> Ye lovers, that can make of sentement;
> In this cas oghte ye be diligent
> To forthren me somwhat in my labour,
> Whether ye ben with the leef or with the flour.
> For wel I wot, that ye han her-biforn
> Of making ropen, and lad awey the corn;
> And I come after, glening here and there,
> And am ful glad if I may finde an ere
> Of any goodly word that ye han left."

The tragedies of the 'Monkes Tale' are taken from the Bible, Apocrypha, Boccaccio, Boëthius, and Dante. Chaucer's own tale, the interrupted 'Sir Thopas,' a burlesque of contemporary romances, and the Canon's 'Yeoman's Tale,' are probably original. Two are from the Italian, the 'Knight's Tale' from the 'Teseide' of Boccaccio, and the 'Clerk's Tale' from Petrarch. The 'Squire's Tale' and the 'Pardoner's' have an Eastern origin, though Chaucer may have derived the latter from 'Cento Novelle Antiche.' Three or four are taken

directly or indirectly from the Latin, and a dozen
or more from the French.

It would be failing in duty and gratitude not to
give some illustrations of the immense value to the
student of the research and commentary before
referred to, and the aid to be derived therefrom
by the general reader. A comprehensive idea of
the peculiar characteristics of Chaucer's genius is to
be found in the third chapter of Professor Ward's
altogether excellent little book already mentioned.
Here many of his defects are justly attributed to
the fashions and customs and limitations of his age;
when women, for example, were wholly subject to
the caprice of their lords; when it was (in literature, at least) regarded as the duty of an ideal wife
to be submissively amiable, even if her brutal husband deprived her of her children, and led her to
think he had destroyed them; when scholasticism
represented sound learning; when intellectual liberty
was almost unknown—these things are answerable
for the absence of literary perspective and for the
pictures of overstrained fidelity to an idea as the
only representative of the healthy morality of a
more enlightened age. The individuality of our
poet being disencumbered of blemishes belonging to
his times, and for which he cannot be held respon-
sible, we are the better able to appreciate those
qualities which are exclusively his own, his exuberant fancy, his gaiety, the brightness of his style,
the melody of his word-music, his joyous pictures of
love and life, his mirth and his humour. The
value of Ten Brink's classification of Chaucer's
writings has been acknowledged. Dr. Furnivall and

the late Henry Bradshaw exhibited the highest
degree of skilled literary labour in their careful investigation of different manuscripts, whereby they
were able to ascertain by internal evidence the correct order in which the ' Canterbury Tales ' should
be arranged ; and Dr. Furnivall's hexapla or six-text
edition of the ' Tales ' has been of value to every
student since its appearance. Of Professor Skeat
it almost might be said that Chaucer is his gift to
the nineteenth century. Many of the poems were
unintelligible before they were subjected to his
scholarly treatment. We have now trustworthy versions of all the works. The separation of the genuine
from the spurious has been accomplished by the
comparative study of contemporary and later language and style, based upon an accurate knowledge
of Middle-English grammar.* Messrs. A. J. Wyatt
and W. H. Low, in their most useful text-book, thus
give the series of tests which any poem attributed
to Chaucer must stand successfully :—(*a*) Chaucer
never rhymes *y* with *ye;* (*b*) he never rhymes words
in which the final *e* is etymological with words in
which it has no etymological force or justification
whatever ; (*c*) he never uses assonances—such as
" shape," " make "—instead of rhymes. (*d*) A
work not written in Eastern Midland dialect cannot
be Chaucer's if, as is usually the case, the marks of
dialect are ineradicable. (*e*) A rhyme-index has
been compiled from Chaucer's certainly genuine
poems, containing all the rhymes that he is known

* See ' The Chaucer Canon,' with a discussion of the Works
associated with the name of Geoffrey Chaucer. By the Rev.
Walter W. Skeat. Oxford, 1900.

to have used. Any poem that satisfactorily passed such negative tests as these must still render sufficient positive evidence to prove that it is not the work of an early imitator. By these and by metrical and other tests, the following poems, formerly admitted, have been rejected from the Chaucer canon :—' The Compleint of the Black Knight,' 'The Cuckoo and the Nightingale,' 'The Court of Love,' 'Chaucer's Dream,' ' The Flower and the Leaf,' etc. Tyrwhitt's analysis of the ' Teseide ' of Boccaccio has facilitated its comparison with ' The Knight's Tale,' and enabled the student to distinguish between " Boccaccio's cumbrous romantic-classic epic and Chaucer's compact romantic story." Mr. A. J. Wyatt, in the introduction to his edition of ' The Knight's Tale,' indicates several of the more marked contrasts which illustrate the superiority of Chaucer's method and style. These are greater directness and rapidity of treatment, more artistic skill, a higher degree of chivalry and poetic justice.

P. W. A.

CHAUCER.

THE POETICAL CONTEMPORARIES OF CHAUCER.

BY H. M. IMBERT-TERRY, F.R.S.L.

FROM time to time the attention of those who are
interested in the science of astronomy has been
excited by the discovery of new luminaries, some of
which, situated in regions vastly distant from this
earth, appear to have their motions swayed by the
mass of immeasurably larger neighbours. It can
well be understood that in these explorations the
interest would be greatly increased if, in the course
of further investigation, the fact became apparent
that the supposed satellites did not in reality
belong to that particular system of which it was
presumed they formed a part, but shone by their
own light.

Whether such an hypothesis is allowable in
astronomy I do not know, but the simile most
appropriately applies to the subject on which I
have the privilege of addressing you this afternoon,
for of the four poetical contemporaries of Chaucer,
" The Morning Star of Song," while two of them
may well be described as satellites—Occleve being
a close and almost slavish imitator of the master,
and Lydgate showing in every way the influence
and inspiration of his superior genius,—yet of the

1

others, one, Gower, gained little or nothing from
his younger contemporary; and the fourth, the
author, whoever he may be, of ' The Vision of Piers
Plowman,' was, both in the source from which he
derived his ideas and the manner in which he dealt
with them, diametrically opposed to him whom
posterity knows as the father of English poetry.

In dealing with the contemporaries of Chaucer,
especially those who lived in England, the fact becomes apparent that Chaucer stood alone, a great
star surrounded by lesser lights whose feeble
twinklings are almost entirely obscured by the
mists of ages ; presenting in this respect a marked
contrast to the somewhat similar phenomena of
Elizabethan times, when a splendid system of
poetic luminaries was revealed, of varying magni-
tudes, no doubt, but all adding something to the
literary constellation.

Greatly as we admire the genius of Chaucer, pre-
eminently as that genius shines out of the poetical
obscurity of his age, yet the fact remains that his
efforts left less mark on the literature of the
period in which he lived, especially in his native
country, than was the case with any other equally
inspired writer.

It was not that his light was deficient in brightness or purity, but that the literary atmosphere
which surrounded him was incapable of assimilating
his beams.

While indeed we may thankfully acknowledge
the many and valuable improvements which Chaucer
made, both in the idiom of the English tongue and
in the metre of English poetry ; while we may

gratefully allow that, as James Russell Lowell admirably observes, " he found that tongue a dialect, and he left it a language;" yet the fact can hardly be denied that the improvements which his genius effected were too far in advance of the national intellect to produce immediate results on the literature of the period; in reality they operated not so much as a stimulus, but as a restraint on the halting muse of his poetical successors.

The true reason of the dearth of good literature immediately after the death of the great poet was not, as has been argued, the disorders of the times, for exciting events have frequently proved an actual impulse to real genius ; but the absolute lack of genuine literary talent, a lack which, to a certain extent, may have been due to the difficulties thrown in the way of composition by the wide diversities of forms of speech which existed in the country during the whole of the fourteenth century, the transition from which into English took place by far less rapid steps than has usually been supposed.

Ranulph Higden, an old Latin chronicler, about the year 1326, wrote his ' Polychronicon,' which was translated into English by John of Trevisa, the chaplain priest and rector of Berkeley, a writer of that age gifted with distinct talent, who, moreover, is credited with having accomplished an English translation of the Bible, a copy of which is supposed, on the authority of Mr. T. F. Dibdin, to exist, or to have existed, in the Vatican library.

Higden in his work declares, "There are four kinds of speech in England, the Northern, the Midland, and the Southern dialects, while by an admixture of Danish and Norman the national tongue is much corrupted; and he further reiterates, as John of Trevisa expresses it, " The langage of the Northumbres, and specyally at Yorke, is so sharpe, slytting, frotyng, and unshape, that we sothern men maye unneth understande that langage; " when, in addition, it is remembered that the idiom of the court was French, and the medium of such literature as existed Latin, it can well be understood that a lengthy period of national education was absolutely necessary before a well-ordered and a concrete language would be unanimously accepted; and we may allow the apology of John Lydgate, who, nearly a hundred years later, declared, by way of excuse for his literary shortcomings,—

> " And I conuersaunte and borne in the partes
> Where my natyfe langage is moost corrupte,
> And with moost sondry tonges myxte and rupte."

But yet among all this confusion, a confusion more confounded by the distress and wars into which the nation had been plunged, there occur many gleams of light, precursors of a brighter and clearer intellectual atmosphere. As an instance of how a modicum of scholarship was permeating the nation in the middle of the fourteenth century, it was asserted by an old chronicler that, according to the returns of the Rolls Court, written signatures instead of crosses or marks became more common; and John of Trevisa distinctly states that, although formerly the children of gentlemen were only taught to speak French, " the manner is since some deal changed; for John Cornwale, a maister of grammar, changed the lore in grammer scoie and construeth of French into English. So now the yere of our Lord 1385, in all the grammar scoles in England, children learneth French and construeth and learneth also Englische."

Before this date, moreover, in the year 1350 or 1352, Laurence Minot, whom Hallam describes as the first original poet in our language, those preceding him being mere translators, wrote his songs of the warlike deeds of King Edward III, the sea fight at Sluys and the expedition into Brabant—

> " Edward, our comely King,
>   In Brabant has his dwelling ; "

being the most popular ; and, perhaps, by thus arousing the metrical instincts of the people, did something towards preparing the national mind for more serious compositions. The songs of Laurence Minot ceased ; the victories which inspired his lays became forgotten and no fresh triumphs were achieved to excite the vulgar fancy ; ten years passed by, years of national dismay and distress. The two great forces which had dominated the twelfth and thirteenth centuries, the discipline of the laws of chivalry and the powerful ordinance of the Roman Church, were both rapidly on the wane, their strength and influence steadily and consistently deteriorating.

With the decline of the Roman prestige, largely caused by the removal of the Papal Court to Avignon and the consequent relaxation of the bonds of eccle-siastical supervision, corruption and disorder spread with great celerity over all parts of the clerical body and especially among the mendicant orders ;

thus the wickedness and lax morality of the clergy, combined with the rapacity and oppression of the Royal purveyors, seizing by force whatever might be considered necessary for the maintenance of a luxurious and overgrown court, powerfully contributed towards creating an almost national spirit of embittered antagonism towards the rulers of the country, whether lay or clerical.

Indeed, at this time, the doings of both nature and men wrought much evil in the land. While the warlike proclivities of the King denuded the country alike of its defenders and its workers, while the heavy subsidies he demanded drained the nation of its resources and its wealth, the convulsions of nature were so extreme as to strike terror into the hearts of a people whose ignorance and superstition rendered them an easy prey to such impulses.

The years 1360 and 1361 were periods of great meteorological activity, violent storms occurring, upsetting trees and destroying buildings, the tower of Norwich Cathedral being levelled by the force of the wind. So fierce was the storm of rain and hail which swept over the centre of France that the English troops, dismayed by its vehemence, dared not attack the crippled and oft-defeated French, and Edward, discomfited and depressed by that which, no doubt, was considered divine intervention, hastened to conclude a peace which, but for the interference of nature, might have been long deferred.

Plague and sickness also spread over the unhappy country, and thus, deprived alike of warlike glories abroad, tempest torn, impoverished and scourged by disease at home, the masses of the people were peculiarly predisposed for any emotional influence which might be brought to bear upon them.

There can be but little doubt that this condition of affairs prompted, at least in some measure, the production of one of the most remarkable poems that has enriched our English literature, a poem, moreover, which certainly was the most considerable composition which existed in our language anterior to the ' Canterbury Tales.'

' Visio Willelmi de Petro le Plowman ; the Vision of William concerning Piers Plowman,' is the title of that which in many ways is an extraordinary work.

At a period when the efforts of all poetical writers were bent on expressing their thoughts by means of the French innovation of rhymed terminations, this allegory of Piers Plowman was written exclusively in the old Saxon alliterative measure ; indeed, as Professor Henry Morley justly observes, " This poem was written for the English people by a poet who not only employed, like Layamon, a Saxon tongue to the utmost, but in whom we again hear the old music of Cædmon's form of verse."

The metre in which the vision was composed, according to Bishop Percy, who has written an essay on the subject, resembled the old alliterative measure of the Icelandic Scalds, which may roughly be described as a verse, with a strong cæsura in the middle, containing, in the first half, two accented words beginning with an identical letter ; which same letter is the initial of one accented syllable in the second half of the measure :

> " Ac on a May morwenhyge,
> On Malverne hilles,
> Me bifel a ferly,
> Of fairye me thoghte.
> I was wery for-wandred,
> And wente me to reste
> Under a brood bank
> By a bournes syde ;
> And as I lay and lenede,
> And loked on the watres,
> I slombred into a slepyng,
> It sweyed so muyre."

In the form of a vision, or rather a series of visions, the favourite contrivance of mediæval authors, the poet describes how

> " A fair feeld ful of folk
> Fond I ther bitwene,
> Of alle menere of men,
> The meene and the riche,
> Werchynge and wandrynge,
> As the world asketh."

This fair field full of folk, not very many indeed in number, for the nation at this time was after all but an inconsiderable people, contained examples of all sorts and conditions of men. Ploughmen and gluttons, courtiers and anchorites, minstrels (musicians, that is to say) ; " as getteth their gold with glee, guiltless I lief ; " and japers and janglers (mountebanks, probably) ; " Judas' children, feigning them fantasies and fools themselves make." Bidders and beggars, bakers and brewsters, pilgrims and pardoners, hinds and highwaymen, all rubbing shoulder, pass before the poet's view and afford much material for caustic satire on the sins and vices to which they were addicted.

Turning with a rapid transition, as was his wont, from a graphic description of homely but natural people, the author depicts the arrival of many allegorical personages.

Dame Holy Church ;

> " A lovely lady of leere,
> In lynnen y-clothed,"

came down from a castle, and instructed the dreamer as regards the new arrivals. A Wedding is about to take place between a fascinating maiden, Mede, or Bribery, and Falsehood, the son of Favel, whose name and character are perhaps best described by the modern expression, Humbug. These, with their appropriate followers, Guile and Liar, &c., are eventually summoned before the King in the Court at Westmynstre and the proceedings which ensue afford great opportunity to the satirist of lashing the many crying evils of the day. The threat of the King that he will hang Falsehood and Favel becoming known to the company, it rapidly disperses ; Guile finding refuge among the merchants and tradespeople :

> " And merchants met with him, and made him abide,
> And shut him in their shoppes to show their wares,
> And parelled him like a prentice, the people to serve."

Liar, because of his tales, was nowhere welcome ;

> " Till pardoners had pity on him, and pulled to house,
> They washed him and wiped him and wound him in
> clouts,
> And sent him on Sunday with seals to the Church."

there he sold pardons for pence until the Friars thought he might be useful and dressed him as one of their order. Eventually he was sent to Rome, where according to the poet he still dwells.

Mede being brought before the King, her charming behaviour made such a favourable impression that the Monarch suggested she should be shriven by a priest and obtain forgiveness for her ill-doings. It is hinted by the reverend confessor that the gift of a painted window to the monastery could but largely conduce to the ultimate salvation of the donor ;

" We have a window a working, which stands us full
    high,
  Will you glaze the gable, and grave there your name,
  In masses and in matins for Mede we will sing,
  Solemnly and soothly as for a sister of our order."

The allegory of the Marriage of Mede and its consequences occupies a considerable portion of the first part of the poem ; but then the author, in his usual manner, suddenly changes his design. A preacher, Repentance, appears and exerts his oratory to such effect that the seven deadly Sins make confession of their guilt and the multitude throngs round the speaker ;

" A thousand of men through thronging together,
  Crying upward to Christ and His clean Mother,
  To have grace to go with Him, Truth to seek."

But, alas, no one knows the way to truth, even a holy Pilgrim, although indeed he had visited Sinai and Bethlehem, Alexandria and Babylon, was feign to declare—

"I seed never Palmer with pick nor with scrip,
   Ask after Truth ever, till now in this place."

Whereupon,

"Peter : quoth a Plowman, and put forth his head,
   I know him as well as a clerk knows his books ; "

and thus, abruptly, Piers the Plowman is brought
upon the scene.

It is one of the peculiarities of this most peculiar
poem that as the book progresses—and there can
be but little doubt that the author spent his lifetime
in writing and revising the composition, three distinct versions of which exist—the nature of Piers,
the chief character, undergoes a great and complete
change.   In the first part he is but a type of the
honest, God-fearing, straightforward workman, in-
tent on doing his duty and determined, as far as his
power permits, to make others do the same.   This
phase of character is so pronounced that for many
years after the poem was written the name Piers
Plowman was used by other authors to indicate any
member of the working classes who was considered
to set an example to his fellows.   Piers refuses to
act as a guide to Truth, for his appointed task is to
sow his half acre, and in defence of his theory that
all who live by bread should work for their bread,
he utters economic opinions which, I fear in the
present day, would hardly conduce to his popularity
among his fellow English labourers ; but in the
second portion of the allegory the scheme of the
vision, as Professor Skeat has shown, completely
changes.   And here it should at once be gratefully
acknowledged that all which is known, or likely to

be known, concerning this remarkable composition is to be found in that monumental work, the three parallel texts of Piers Plowman, edited by the distinguished Anglo-Saxon scholar whose name has just been mentioned and whose labours in this direction have earned for him the warmest thanks of all true lovers of English literature.

Instead of the vivid scenes of homely life with which the poet formerly dealt, in the latter portion of his task he writes a long and somewhat involved allegory, the life of Dowel, Dobet (or better) and Dobest; an allegory which I cannot help thinking was, at least, the English fount and origin of that terror of childhood, Bunyan's ' Pilgrim's Progress.'

Here the Plowman appears in his final character, step by step his nature expands and becomes idealised, until at last we have the definite announcement that he is Christ the Saviour;

" But Piers the Plowman, Petrus id est Christus."

Without his help charity can never be seen; he alone perceives the secret thoughts of men, and—as the poet has before told us in words, which, considering the age he lived in, are of rare poetical beauty—above all is he sent to the beggars and misshapen people, to the blind, the bedridden, and the broken in their members—in short, to those to whom—

" For love of their low hearts, our Lord hath them granted,
Their penance and their purgatory here on this earth."

Although in this ' Vita de Dowel ' and its sequel the author introduces some of his more homely characters—especially Hawkin the active man, in his clothes soiled with many spots of mud, a type of those busy people who have no time to improve their habits or attend to their soul's health—yet, as a rule, this division of the poem is reflective and even metaphysical, with the usual result that the writer, who, when he spoke of that which he knew and comprehended, wrote lucidly and clearly, in this concluding portion is often involved, obscure and not infrequently prolix and turgid. Yet from the beginning to end the work bears the marks of the deepest earnestness of purpose—the one great labour, as perhaps the one great solace of the author's life. The author! and who was he?

In speaking of the book before hardly mentioning the maker, I follow the example of Mons. Jusserand who, in his charming essay, 'Piers Plowman : a contribution to the History of English Mysticism,' has wittily observed, "Our excuse for putting 'la charrue avant les bœufs' must be that there are no 'bœufs.'" We put the cart before the horse, because we hardly know where to find the animal.

No contemporary writer has mentioned or even hinted at the name of the author of 'Piers Plowman.' The only evidence we possess of his identity is as follows. On the Ashburnham MS. of the poem, in an old hand, is written, "Robert or William Langland made Pers Plowman;" also, on another MS. preserved in Dublin, the following Latin inscription is traced, in characters which are said to be of the fifteenth century. "Memorandum : Quod Stacy de Rokayle pater Willielmi de

Langland, qui Stacius fuit generosus et mora batur in Sheptone under Whicwode, tenens domini Le Spenser in comitatu Oxon. ; qui predictus Willielmus fecit librum qui vocatur Perys Ploughman."

In reference to the difference between the name of the father in this entry, Stacy de Rokayle, and that of the son William Langland, it is interesting to note that the author himself of 'Piers Plowman,' in the following lines distinctly implies that sons did not necessarily take their father's surnames.

"That is not reasonable nor right, to refuse my father's
      surname,
   Since I his son and servant sue for his right."

In addition to the above evidence, such as it is, in a book called the 'Catalogue of Illustrious Writers,' compiled by John Bale, Bishop of Ossory, about the year 1549, there is a long and somewhat erroneous entry. "Robert Langland, priest, composed the 'Visionem Petri Aratoris.' He was born in the county of Salop, in a village commonly called Mortimer Cleobury, which is situate eight miles from the Malvern Hills." No authorities are given for these statements, and no authorities are to be found. The name of Langland is not once mentioned by any contemporary writer, but in the poem itself a remarkable line occurs which could hardly have been included without some special purpose.

"I have Lived in londe, quoth I ; my name is long Wille."

This, if read backwards—a not uncommon species of anagram—gives the name Wille Longlond.

Perhaps, as is the case in all early literature, some information concerning the author may be gleaned from his own work. It therefore is possible that he was born in or about the year 1331, for he tells us his birth took place forty-five winters before the writing of the poem, the special version of which containing the allusion was, as internal evidence shows, undoubtedly composed about the year 1376-77. He also states, "my father and my friends founded me to schole," from which place he presumably was received into the Orders of the Church, for he frequently speaks of his tonsure and his long clothes, once declaring specifically—

"And I live in London; and on London both
The looms I labour with and life load deserve
Is Paternoster and my prymer, placebo and dirige,
And my Psalter some time and my seven psalms,
Thus I sing for the souls of such as me helpen."

In all probability he was one of those singers of the minor orders of the Church, who gained a living by chanting masses and penitential psalms for the souls of the ancestry and friends of such holy people as liked to sedulously practise religion, vicariously, by the help of paid deputies.

He mentions also "Kitte my wife," and "Kalotte," or Nicolette, my daughter, and a little cot in Cornhill; but after all, the information concerning him, which can be gleaned from ulterior evidence or the internal authority of his own writing, is very scanty and dim; and, notwithstanding, from this data both Professor Skeat and

Mons. Jusserand have elaborated most interesting lives of the poet, with every respect for the erudition and imaginative activity of these distinguished scholars, I cannot help agreeing with Mr. Courthope, who on this subject emphatically declares, " For my part, I do not think it desirable to introduce even the appearance of scientific reasoning into what must necessarily always remain a region of nebular hypothesis." One thing, at least, is certain, Langland, or whatever the poet's name may have been, was a man of considerable knowledge and no mean literary skill. Yet, whatever may have been his attainments, it can hardly have been possible for this poor Saxon clerk, as presumably he was, to have read the one work which most vividly recalls his own composition—the great Italian allegory, the ' Divina Commedia ' of Dante Alighieri.

Perhaps, indeed, the resemblance is not difficult to account for. The actual form of a vision was a contrivance common to all early literature, while the miseries and vices which were undermining the social fabric of the times, appealing with equal intensity to both writers, stung into activity the literary genius which existed alike in each of them. It was the similarity of the problem to be solved which caused a resemblance in the attempted solution; calling forth in both cases the work most suited for dealing with the evil. And yet in Langland's poem this very suitability of manner is one of the chief literary defects. In Dante's great allegory, the work of a man of noble birth, mingling with the ruling classes of his day, master of a musical tongue and of a beautiful form of verse, the whole machinery of the vision, the terrible crimes and the more terrible punishments, are thrilling, mystic and awe inspiring ; but on the other hand, the Englishman, living among low bred and abject people, writing in an unformed language and in an archaic metre, which even then had almost become obsolete, was obliged, perforce, to appeal by a rough and homely strain to the uneducated and unrefined audience which surrounded him. Thus the familiar types, the low level of the actors in Piers Plowman, seem to render the contrivance of a vision unnecessary and even incongruous ; indeed, to this old English composition might even more appropriately be applied the remark made by an American critic of commonplace tendencies concerning ' Dante's Inferno : ' " Ah, if he had had to do with my Irish helps, he wouldn't have had to dream dreams."

I cannot help thinking that the author of ' Piers Plowman ' must himself have felt this incongruity, and while he employed the idea of a vision as a shield from the wrath of those whose anger would have been aroused by his relentless satire, in his later life, when, as was indubitably the case, he revised and largely re-wrote his poem, he recognised the necessity of carrying out more thoroughly the idea of a mystic scheme, and so concluded his labour with a distinct allegorical and metaphysical discourse, which to a certain extent, was not a logical sequel to his earlier efforts. Vigorous in treatment and strongly national in subject as is William's Dream, certain portions of the poem are undoubtedly influenced by contemporary foreign

2

authors, that perennial source of all thirteenth and fourteenth century literature, the ' Romaunt of the Rose ' being obviously laid under contribution, the character of the Friar Fals Semblant being the original of many of Langland's personages, while the Procession of the Seven Deadly Sins bears a marked resemblance to a similar incident in Roteboeuf's popular satire, ' La Voie de Paradis.' It is also probable, as certain coincidences occur in the works of both authors, that Langland had become acquainted with the celebrated series of visions, ' La Pelegrinage de la Vie Humaine, de l'Ame et de Jesu Christ,' which were composed in 1330, by Guillaume de Deguiville, and which were certainly known in England at this period, a Hymn to the Virgin by the French poet having been translated into English by no less a person than Chaucer himself.

There can be no doubt also that the writer of ' Piers Plowman ' had read diligently a book greatly in request in the Middle Ages, the ' Gospel of Nicodemus,' a curious romance, said to be forged by the early Greek writers in Constantinople, of which an English translation by John of Trevisa existed in the fourteenth century.

The prologue to this gospel, to which many a writer of times of chivalry was indebted for his material, in the edition printed by Wynkyn de Worde in 1509, was as follows : " It befel in the nineteenth year of Tilbury Caesar, Emperor of Rome, in the Seignourie of Herod, this time Joseph and Annas were Lords above all Justices, Mayors and Jews ; Nicodemus which was a worthy prince did write this blessed story in Hebrew, and Theodosias did translate it out of Hebrew into Latin, and Bishop Turpin did translate it out of Latin into French, and hereafter ensueth the blessed story."

From the aforesaid story Langland borrowed the whole incident of the 'Joust of Jesus,' where the Saviour of Mankind, habited in the helm and hauberk of human nature, which belonged to Piers Plowman, did battle with the Fiend and his emissary Falsedoom-to-die.

But apart from these resemblances which, after all, are common to all mediæval literature, much of which was primarily drawn from identical sources, the work of this English poet, contemporary with Chaucer, is remarkable for the strong individuality and keen originality both of its conception and its execution.

It was thought by the older school of critics that Langland wrote in a dialect containing a far greater admixture of Anglo-Saxon than that used by Chaucer, Isaac Disraeli even saying that the appellation of "pure well of English undefiled," which Spenser applies to Chaucer would be more fittingly given to Langland. With all respect to this delightful commentator, his assertion has now been proved not to be the case. Both of these poets wrote in the language in common use in their day, and, indeed, quite as many French words are to be found in 'Piers Plowman' as in the 'Canterbury Tales.' "Porta-tif," "percant as a needle," "she mercied him gratefully," "he manged muchly," being examples taken at random from the first few pages of the satire.

Of the immense popularity of the work there can be no doubt. Forty-five MSS. of Piers Plowman are now in existence, and bibliographical authorities tell of at least two more which must have been seen and handled. The poem written for the Commons, the hero a son of the soil, instinct with the feelings and prejudices of his class, became a very watchword among the peasantry; the secret letter of the seditious priest, John Ball, containing a quotation from this work as a rallying cry for his followers. The religious opinions also of the author conduced to extend this popularity even into generations remote from his own. At the time of the Reformation certain lines which occur in the poem were, by the zeal of the Reformers, converted into prophetic utterances.

" And there shall come a King and confess you religious,
   And beat you as the Bible telleth for breaking of your
      rule,
   And amend you monials, monks and canons,
   For the Abbot of Abingdon and the Abbess his niece,
   Shall have knock of a King and incurable the wound,
   And when the King come as chronicles me told,
   Clerks and Holy Church shall be clothed anew."

These words, remarkable no doubt from one who was a clerk and a Churchman, were hailed by the acidulated controversalists of the reign of Edward VI as the inspired warnings of a very prophet denouncing divine judgment against a forsaken Church; but it is not by any means certain that the writer of these verses, at the time they were penned, was in reality giving vent to any specially new or far-reaching doctrine. Henry Bolingbroke, the man of the times to whom all reformers turned their eyes, is reported to have held very free opinions regarding the temporal possessions of the Church, and it is probable that other great nobles entertained the same views, that to adjust the proper equilibrium of the nation, the struggling State should take whatever was necessary for its requirements from an opulent and overgrown hierarchy. Langland tells us that he frequently sought invitations to the tables of the great. A somewhat prolonged political experience teaches me that it is not unreasonable to suppose he may have imbibed the political opinion of his hosts at the same time as he enjoyed their hospitality. Langland, indeed, at the period of the Reformation, was credited with being a Wickliffite; but here again a mistake has been made, for although he strongly condemned and satirised the corruption of the friars and other ecclesiastical orders, yet he was, as is frequently apparent in his poem, a strong upholder of the dignity and authority of the Papal office, severely as he might censure the personal frailties of the individual occupier of the Chair of St. Peter. In no sense does he ever support the express doctrine of Wickliffe, that it is incumbent on moral men to refuse religious obedience to an immoral leader.

The strong and religious sense of justice with which the book is pervaded no doubt contributed largely to its phenomenal popularity, the title, ' Piers Plowman '—for the author's name is never mentioned—being quoted in almost every composition issued in the two succeeding centuries. ' The Festival of Love,' by Thomas Usk, who was executed in 1388, a very early specimen of English prose, has a reference to this poem in one of its first texts, while Lydgate and Gavin Douglas also allude to it.

Skelton, too, both in the ' Bowge of Court ' and in ' Colin Clout ' often imitates his fourteenth century brother satirist, concerning whom nearly every member of the school of criticism which sprung up in the reign of Elizabeth—Puttenham, Meres, and William Webbe—has something eulogistic to say, the remarks of the last-named especially being worthy of remembrance : " The next of our antient poets that I can tell of I suppose to be Piers Plowman, who in his day is somewhat harsh and obscure, but indeed a very pithy writer, and, to his commendation I speak it, was the first that I have ever seen that observed the quantity of our verse without the curiosity of rhyme."

Gascoigne, in his ' Steel Glass,' the first poem in the English language written in blank verse, and Spenser in the ' Shepherd's Calendar,' both allude either to this poem or ' Piers the Plowman's Crede,' one of its not infrequent imitations ; while Drayton, Fuller, and the author of the old comedy ' A Knack to know a Knave,' are all familiar with the book. Even Milton also quotes it as the earliest satire in English literature, and while writing his description of the lazar-house may even have borne in mind the account which is to be found in Langland's old allegory of Nature sending forth diseases at the bidding of Conscience.

On the last page of a MS. of 'Piers Plowman,' which is preserved in the Cambridge University Library, a copy of another poem has been found, written in the same handwriting, and having all appearance of being composed about the same date as the preceding composition. This poem, which deals with the events of the latter years of Richard II's reign, was printed as far back as 1839 by Mr. Wright, for the Camden Society, under the title of 'A Poem on the Deposition of King Richard II.' Since then, however, Professor Skeat has demonstrated—and the proof, I believe, has universally been accepted—that this work, the initial lines of which are " Now Richard the Rede-less," and which, consequently, has been called by that title, is undoubtedly the work of William, the author of 'Piers Plowman.'

The phraseology, the metre, and the spirit of satire here displayed are all strongly reminiscent of the writer of the earlier work, while the power of the composition is such as to demonstrate that it must, in all circumstances, have been written by a master hand.

Although the poem is short, it contains many spirited and graphic scenes, one of which, the re-ception of Wisdom by the curled and pampered exquisites of the court of Richard, is considered by Professor Skeat as a most striking and forcible satire ; the sarcasm by which the dresses themselves, extravagant almost to grotesqueness, are substi-tuted for the men, unworthy of the name, who wore them, is particularly happy in its effect :

"Let us slay him, quoth the *sleeves which slid upon the earth*,
And all the beardless bairns, bayed on him ever,
And scorned him, for his slaveyn (mantle) was of the
old shape."

The account also of Parliament voting subsidies,
which the obedient majority dare not refuse,
although the process is most distasteful to them, is
a witty piece of character-sketching which might
even apply to a later period than the year *thirteen*
hundred and ninety-nine:

"Comliche (eloquently) a clerk than comsid (began) the
wordis,
And pronouncid the poyntis aparte to hem alle,
And meved ffor money more than ffor out ellis,
     *   *   *   *
Than satte summe as siphre doth in awgrym,
That noteth a place and no thing availith;
     *   *   *   *
And somme were tituleris (talebearers), and to the
Kyngs wente,
And fformed him of foos that good ffrendis weren,
That bablid (spoke) ffor the best. . . .
     *   *   *   *
And somme mafflid with the mouth and nyst what they
mente;
And somme had hire and helde ther-with euere,
And wolde no fforther affoot ffor ffer of her maistris;
And some were so soleyne and sad of her wittis,
That er they come to the clos acombrid they were,
That thei the conclucioun than constrewe ne couthe
(That they the conclusion could neither explain nor
understand)."

In the middle of a sentence the poem ends

abruptly; perhaps because the news of the murder
of the King formed a tragic but logical peroration ;
perhaps because the poet himself died or had no
heart to write further. Who can tell ? The broken
and mysterious ending after all is the most fitting
termination to the broken and mysterious record of
a great soul.

But if the life, the career, and the ending of
Langland are all shrouded in doubt, the same can
hardly be said of the other famous poet who lived
contemporary with him and Chaucer. Of the poet
Gower, Moral Gower, as he is called, we have ample
evidence that he lived, flourished, and died, in the
splendid tomb which has been raised to his memory
within the church which he loved and enriched,
St. Saviour's, Southwark, where he lies, with the
marks of royal favour and literary appreciation
around him, his head reposing on three ponderous
tomes of his own composition, the contents of
which, perhaps, may have contributed to the
severely comatose expression which still rests on
his countenance. For whatever great and good
qualities may be allowed to Gower's muse, the
quality of conciseness or brilliancy can hardly be
included.

With the exception of some French ballades,
presumably written when he was a young man,
which show distinct elegance of thought and execution, the only known writings of Gower are three
long poems, 'Speculum Meditantis,' 'Vox Clamantis,' and 'Confessio Amantis.' The first
was, it is believed—for no trace of it now remains
—a long didactic treatise, written in French, on the

general nature of virtue and vice, chiefly as exemplified in conjugal fidelity and the reverse. The second, 'Vox Clamantis,' is a Latin chronicle of the popular tumults in the early days of the reign of Richard II. But the fame of Gower rests, and rightly rests, on his great English poem, the 'Confessio Amantis,' a work, as he states in the first editions, written at the request of the King, Richard, but written not in courtly French or in clerkly Latin, but in the rising vernacular tongue of the people, the English language.

> " Som may like of what I write ;
> And that for fewé men endite,
> In our Englisshe I thenké make
> A boké for Englandés sake."

As it was in the fourteenth, so happily for English literature it was also in the fifteenth and sixteenth centuries. The same desire to render the English tongue, rude, rough as it then sounded, a fitting medium for a national literature spurred English writers on in their endeavour to improve and polish their native language. What Gower began in 1386 Skelton continued in 1500.

> " The English tongue is rude, and hard to be enneued,
> That I would apply to write ornately,
> I know not where to find terms to serve my mind."

Thus the task proceeded ; after Skelton, Ascham, against his scholarly instinct, wrote his first treatise, 'Toxophilus,' in the vulgar tongue, forming a corner-stone in the glorious edifice of vernacular

literature which adorned the great days of Queen
Elizabeth.

Whether or no Gower really wrote his chief work
at the express command of the King is open to
doubt, but at least the fact is certain that, unlike
Langland, whose origin was perhaps obscure,
whose sympathies were certainly with the people,
Gower was well born, at a time when good birth
was a valuable commodity, well educated, and well
endowed with worldly goods.

Caxton, in his first edition of the poet's writings,
has announced that John Gower was a squire born
in Wales in the time of Richard II. As Richard
did not ascend the throne until 1377, and Gower
died an old and blind man in 1408, this information
is obviously inaccurate; indeed, it has been
tolerably well ascertained that this early English
writer was a gentleman of Kent, possessing considerable landed estates in Suffolk and other
counties, portions of which he left, as his will
proves, to his widow, Agnes Grundoff, the wife of
his old age.

Born some years before Chaucer, living eight
years longer—a passive existence, indeed, crippled
and blind,—Gower's life derives additional interest
from the fact that in many ways it was closely connected with his illustrious contemporary. In 1378,
when Chaucer left England for the Continent, he
appointed Gower as his attorney or deputy in the
Controllership of the Customs, the personal friendship being evidently supplemented by literary
appreciation, as in the poem, 'Troilus and
Cressida,' he speaks with admiration of Gower's

talents, and gives the epithet which has designated the old poet through centuries, " Oh, moral Gower, this book I direct to thee."

Gower returns the compliment in the Epilogue to the ' Confessio Amantis ' by making Venus greet Chaucer as her favoured follower :

> " And grete well Chaucer, when ye mete,
>   As my disciple and my poete.
>   For in the flourés of his youth,
>   In sondry wise, was he well couth
>   Of ditties and of songés glade,
>   The which he for my saké made."

Alas ! the amicable relationship between those two celebrated poets was not of very long duration. Indeed, so great must have been the disparity of disposition between the vivacious and mercurial Chaucer and the didactic and sententious Gower, that the fact that terms of friendship ever existed between them is a testimony, at least, to the liberality of their opinions. For while sufficient evidence—positive and presumptive—exists to show that Chaucer did not lead the life of an anchorite, Gower is nothing if not moral, dogmatic, and precise; while, above all, he is singularly deficient in that most lovable characteristic of Chaucer, an affection for the sounds and sights of nature. As the celebrated Charles James Fox observed, " Chaucer of all poets is fondest of the singing of birds." Great as were the aims of Gower, valuable as were the services he rendered as a pioneer in English literature, it cannot be justly contended that his genius was strong or his inspiration divine.

Mons. Taine, in his 'History of Literature,' has, in his usual epigrammatic manner, well insisted on this fact :—" The poor little poetic spring flows yet in thin transparent streamlets over smooth pebbles, and murmurs with a babble so low that at times you cannot hear it."

This indeed may be true, but even such a distinguished writer as M. Taine might perhaps have deigned to remember that in a literary Sahara such as existed in those days, even a trickling streamlet was, to those who passed by, a source of sustenance and renewed vigour. That Gower helped to refine and enlarge the language is now admitted; even if this were all the service he rendered, it alone entitles him to our gratitude and respect.

However, we must not quarrel with the epigrammatist, especially in the present day, when the intellectual laziness of the nineteenth century is such that we all like to get our information compressed in an epigram, as some of us prefer to take our pills enveloped in patent capsules.

With all his limitations Gower has great and varied talents. Warton, whose opinion commands at least respectful attention, declares that if Chaucer had not existed the compositions of Gower would by themselves have been sufficient to rescue the reigns of Edward III and Richard II from the imputation of barbarism.

The 'Vox Clamantis, or the Voice of one Crying,' is a poem of power. The fact, however, that it is written in Latin elegiacs neutralises altogether its value as far as the literature of this country is concerned ; but the great English work, the 'Confessio Amantis,' has left an indelible mark in the annals of poetic composition.

Possibly Chaucer borrowed from it the idea of his 'Man of Law's Tale,' the story of which is identical with the episode of Constantia in Gower's poem; and even Shakespeare may perhaps have been also indebted to the old bard for the incident of the three caskets, so admirably introduced into the 'Merchant of Venice,' although in the latter case it is also possible that a still older source had been tapped, the 'Gesta Romanorum' itself.

Judged by critical standards, Gower is undoubtedly the most literary of Chaucer's contemporaries; his verse, though somewhat archaic in form, being both polished and fluent. He possesses, notwithstanding what old Puttenham calls "peevish affectations," some considerable powers of imagination and even dramatic description; but yet in the essence of true poetry he is markedly deficient. His muse is always fettered, his poetic desires are curbed by most rigid restraints; never once does he indulge, or appear to wish to indulge, in that luxury—the greatest of all to a true poetic mind—the luxury of unbridled sentiment. He speaks of love, the 'Confessions of a Lover to Genius,' but the discourse chiefly turns on the nature of the seven deadly sins, with an occasional incident in the career of celebrated, if mythological, personages whose affections have been recorded in ancient literature, beginning with Adam and Eve, and including Tristan and Isolde, Jason and Creusa, Samson and Delilah, Aristotle, with the Queen of Greece and Nebuchadnezzar. The exact nature of the amorous proclivities of the last-named is not, however, enlarged upon. The treatment of the subject is exhaustive, the poem containing some thirty thousand lines, into which a large amount of erudition has been crammed, the poet treating of chemistry, politics, and philosophy as the natural concomitants of a loving disposition. But even with all this fund of information the ordinary reader will at least sympathise with the Lover, who, in the midst of one of the most elaborate disquisitions of Genius, somewhat mournfully remarks, " The tale soundeth in mine ear, but yet mine heart is elsewhere." Needless to say, the work abounds in odd anachronisms. For instance, Ulysses, the Grecian hero, who is described as a clerk, obtains his knowledge of varied accomplishments from somewhat strange sources, the prophet Daniel being his instructor in divination, Zoroaster in magic ; Noah, Abraham, and Moses are cited as the chief authorities on the important science of astrology. It is surely a regrettable omission that the first-named patriarch was not also mentioned as an adept in the art of navigation.

Yet, with every fault of omission or commission, to Gower is justly due the credit of being the first author in English literature who wrote a connected series of tales ; the scheme of the ' Confessio Amantis ' being admittedly but a framework on which to hang a sequence of anecdotes culled from widely different sources.

The idea of joining together entertaining narratives is undoubtedly very old, and was probably derived from the East; but the authors to whom

Gower was indebted both for his plan and much of his material were, it is needless to say, Boccaccio and Jean de Meung, although in the excerpts he borrowed from the ' Romaunt of the Rose ' it is only fair to remark that he omitted much of the bitter invective with which Jean de Meung embellished the original work of Guillaume de Loris.

Gower, indeed, is a good story-teller, but it is in the original parts of his poems that his lack of imagination is chiefly discernible. Graces of style, neatness of execution, in almost every form of art may not only produce good work, but may even effect a useful advance in a special direction ; but with regard to poetry, the oft-quoted line of Horace is still true. Poetry is not tolerable unless it bears the golden stamp of genius. Happily the features of genius are not all cast in the same mould ; indeed, the very essence of what is commonly called genius demands spontaneity and variety. The world would be very dull were all its poets Miltons ; but, grave or gay, poetry, to be true poetry, must spring from the inborn nature of the poet, and not be simply manufactured by rules of art.

It is this fact which renders criticism of these early authors so difficult. Neither Gower, Occleve, Lydgate, nor, in truth, any poet who existed in England until the reign of Elizabeth, with the exception of Chaucer, possessed the true poetic inspiration. And this is specially true of those who immediately succeeded the author of the ' Canterbury Tales.'

The first in point of succession, Occleve, indeed has only one claim to recognition—that he con-

sidered Chaucer as his teacher, and perpetuated the
memory of the great poet by causing to be drawn
on the margin of his principal poem, ' The Governail of Princes,' now in the British Museum, a
portrait of the master whose disciple he was well
content to be.

> " But weylewey ! so is myn hert(e) wo,
>   That the honour of Englyssh tongue is deed,
>   Of which I wont was han conseil and reed.
> O maister deere and fadir reuerent,
>   Mi maister Chaucer, flour of eloquence,
> Mirour of fructuous entendement,
>   O vniversel fadir in science."

This poet, born, it may be believed, about 1368–9
at Occlif, in Bedfordshire, was brought up for the
priesthood, but thought better of it :

> " I whilom thought to have been a priest,
>   Now past is the race."

So he entered, as a clerk, the Privy Seal Office, the
chief secretary of which at that time was always an
ecclesiastic ; and when his salary fell into arrears,
which seems to have been its normal condition, he
wrote an ode or a dialogue to some distinguished
person, apparently as a hint that the writer was
still alive and wished to remain so.

Halting as is the muse of Occleve—" a cold genius
and a feeble writer," says Warton ; " wretchedly
bad, abounding with pedantry and destitute of all
grace and spirit," declares Hallam,—yet scant
justice has been done even to him by the school of
critics of the last century, of whom Ritson and

3

Ellis were the chiefs. The short poems in which
Occleve wrote mainly about himself, and his not too
reputable mode of living, are curious mementos of
the men and manners of the period, and as such
possess a distinct value. In one poem at least,
' The Mother of God,' he has taken higher ground ;
for many years this hymn was attributed to
Chaucer and published among his minor compositions, but since that time the Phillips MSS. have
been discovered, in one of which this poem was
found not only written in Occleve's own handwriting, but included among compositions of which he
distinctly was the author. From this fact, and the
internal evidence of the workmanship, the best
authorities have decided to attribute the hymn to
Occleve, and not to Chaucer.

In 1796 Mr. Mason printed six of Occleve's auto-
biographical poems, six " of peculiar stupidity," as
Mr. Ritson genially remarks. To these, and to one
especially, ' Le Male Regle,' we are indebted for such
knowledge of the author as we possess.

He confesses to a predilection for the good things
of life :

> " Reson me bad and redde as for the beste,
>   To ete and drynke in tyme attemprely."

But he rejects the good advice, and frequents the
tavern at Paul's in very good-looking but somewhat
shameless female company :

> " That so goodly so shaply were, and feir,
>   And so plesant of port and of maneere,
>   And of Atyr passyngly wel byseye,

Ther was sweet wyn ynow thurgh-out the hous,
And wafres thikke for this conpaignie
That I spak of been sumwhat likerous,
Where as they mowe a draght of wyn espie,
Sweete and in wirkynge hoot for the maistrie
To warme a stomak with ther-of they dranke.
To suffre hem paie, had been no courtesie :
That charge I tooke to wynne loue and thanke."

Indeed, this fifteenth century civil servant seems
to have had some very modern failings ; he was fond
of swaggering at hostelries at Westminster Gate,
and always paid the cooks all they asked :

" I pynchid nat at hem in myn acate,
But paied hem as that they axe wolde ;
Wherefore I was the welcomere algate,
And for 'a verray gentil man' y-holde."

He liked the flattery, and so " When I depart
sholdé and go my way Home to the privy seal," he
would take a boat, which he could ill afford, but
could not deny himself the pleasure of posing as a
great man :

" Othir than 'maistir' callid was I neuere,
Among this meynee, in myn audience.
Me thoghte I was y-maad a man for euere :
So tikelid me that nyce reuerence."

These lines show the strong influence which
Chaucer had exercised over his pupil ; as Professor
Skeat observes, " if Occleve learnt nothing else, he
certainly learnt the true scansion of the poet's lines,
and imitated his metres and his rhymes with great
exactness."

Occleve's chief work was called ' De Regimine Principium, or the Governail of Princes,' being compiled from a philosophical treatise spuriously attributed to Aristotle, entitled ' Secretum Secretorum,' a very favourite source of inspiration for old authors, Gower having already tapped the fount to supply the seventh book of his ' Confessio Amantis.' But the whole of Occleve's works, as well as, to a great extent, the writings of his better known contemporary Lydgate, show but too well that the impetus given by Chaucer to the literature of the fourteenth century had almost expended its force.

Happily the taste for letters remained, a keen desire being displayed by the rulers of this country to create and maintain a national literature.

It has usually been supposed that the first authors by profession, living—or rather starving— on the proceeds of their pens, were the University wits in the reign of Elizabeth,—Green, Peele, Marlowe, Nashe, &c. ; but, from his own showing, John Lydgate, the monk of Bury, is really entitled to this distinction.

Born in 1371, at Lydgate, near Newmarket—" I was born at Lydgate, where Bacchus liquer doth full scarsely flow,"—he entered, when young, the Benedictine monastery at Bury St. Edmunds, and soon commenced a literary career which, terminating only with his life, is a record of voluble industry, 114 works of this voluminous writer being still known, and probably an equal number having been lost in the lapse of ages. There are reasons to suppose that Lydgate's first literary efforts took the form of allegories, his ' Court of Sapience ' and

'Temple of Glass,' both presumably published before the year 1411, being of this character. But, in truth, the author was as adaptable as indefatigable ; 'Lives of Saints,' 'Classic Epics,' a 'Dance of Death,' and a ballad of London life, 'Simon Lickpenny' (Lackpenny), are but a few of the outpourings from his versatile pen.

He was commissioned by Abbot Wheathampstead to write a life of St. Alban, and in 1426 he appeared in Paris, translating into English doggrel a poetical pedigree by Laurence Callot, which proved that Henry VI was the rightful heir to the throne of France to the complete exclusion of all other pretenders. But before this time he had gained influential patrons ; in 1412, at the command of Prince Henry, he undertook the imposing task of metrically translating the 'History of Troy,' a romance of 30,000 lines by Guido di Colonna. In the performance of this labour, which took him eight years more or less, he used the French paraphrase of Laurent de Premierfait, and then with undiminished energy turned his attention to the 'Story of Thebes,' an old troubadour's lay, also used by the aforesaid Guido di Colonna, and probably primarily derived from the epic of Statius. The prologue to this work is in direct imitation of the 'Canterbury Tales;' the author travelling to the shrine of St. Thomas joins Chaucer's celebrated company, and relates this anecdote for their delectation. His appearance, on his showing, does not invite confidence :

> " In a cope of black, and not of grene,
>   On a palfray, slender, long and lene,

> With a rusty bridle, made not for the sale,
> My man toforne with a void male."

The fact that these classic legends of Troy and
Thebes had again become popular throws an interesting light on the literary history of the times,
as demonstrating the revival of a taste for the old
romantic stories of chivalry. As Lydgate apparently knew no Greek, he derived his information
on these subjects from the paraphrase of Guido di
Colonna, and clothing the ancient histories with the
manners of mediæval knight-errantry, he trans-
muted them into feudal romances. The siege of
Troy is but a military operation of the Crusades,
all the engines then employed being called into
requisition; supplemented, however, by the startling
and unexpected addition of brass guns. Lydgate
also gives us the interesting information that the
game of chess was invented by the inhabitants of
the beleaguered city to wile away the tedium of the
siege :

> " Then was found by clerks full prudent
> Of the chess the play most glorius,
> Which is so subtle and so marvellous."

In the year 1426, when in Paris, the busy poet
was commanded by his patron the Earl of Salisbury
to translate Deguiville's lengthy allegory ' Le Pèle-
rinage de la Vie humaine,' to which allusion has
already been made in connection with ' Piers Plowman.' The reduction into English of a poem of
22,000 lines would have supplied, it might justly be
thought, sufficient occupation for the pen of even

such a ready writer as the monk of Bury; but so intense was the desire of members of the Royal Family to increase at least the quantity of English literature, that with scarce an interval Humphrey Duke of Gloucester commissioned the old author to render metrically into the vernacular Boccaccio's work ' De Casibus Virorum Illustrium,' or ' The Fall of Princes,' to call it by the name afterwards given to it. A portion of this composition had already been utilised by Chaucer in the Monk's Tale, and the prospect of re-writing the book seems to have at last struck horror to the wearied soul of Lydgate, now over sixty years of age:

> " Thus my self remembryng on this boke,
>   It to translate how I had undertake,
> Full pale of chere, astonyed in my loke,
>   Mine hand gan tremble, my penne I felt(e) quake."

It appears from old documents that during the years required for the operation of concocting the 36,000 lines which comprised this undertaking, a new prior was elected to the monastery at Hatfield Regis in place of the poet, who had nominally presided there since 1423; and in 1434, four years before he had completed his gigantic task, he once more retired to the home of his childhood at Bury St. Edmunds, where he stayed until his death, which seems to have occurred, appropriately enough, just as he was deeply immersed in a translation of the ' Secretum Secretorum.' Of Lydgate as a writer it is difficult to speak justly; to really criticise the 130,249 lines which he wrote, apart from smaller poems and those of doubtful authenticity, is now

impossible : to quote a well-known line, " Cavil we
may, but never criticise."

Ritson, who devotes twenty-one pages of ' Biblio-
graphia Poetica ' to this author, and who, as old
Gifford said, " always reviews, as the ancients
planted basil, with cursing and swearing," calls the
luckless poet " a voluminous, prosaic, and drivelling
monk, who disgraces the name of his Maister
Chaucer." On the other hand, a greater than
Ritson, the accomplished and elegant poet Gray,
spoke in terms of commendation of his ancient
brother, and even went so far as to declare of
Lydgate, that in choice of expression and smooth-
ness of his verse he far surpassed Gower or
Occleve.

In the opinion of writers who lived in times not
far removed from his own, there is but one opinion
of the monk of Bury,—that he was a fitting asso-
ciate for his master Chaucer, and worthy to have
his name coupled with that great poet for all time.

Skelton, Hawes, and the Elizabethan critics
Puttenham and William Webbe, not only eulogise
his works, but always join his name with his more
illustrious contemporary ; while Tom Nashe, in his
preface to Greene's ' Menaphon,' linking Chaucer,
Gower, and Lydgate together, declares, " One
thing I am sure of, that each of these three have
vaunted their metre with as much admiration in
English as ever the proudest Ariosto did his verse
in Italian." To come to modern times, S. T. Coleridge prefers Lydgate to the " worthless Gower;"
and Mrs. Barrett Browning expresses the distinct
opinion that ' Piers Plowman,' Chaucer's ' House

of Fame,' Lydgate's ' Temple of Glass,' and Hawes'
' Pastime of Pleasure ' are the four columnar mar-
bles, the four allegorical poems, on whose founda-
tion is exalted into light the great allegorical poem
of the world, Spenser's ' Fairy Queen.'

But yet, in my humble opinion, it must be con-
fessed that the writings of Occleve and Lydgate
most unmistakably demonstrate that the innova-
tions which Chaucer introduced into English poetry
were too far advanced for the intellect of the age.
Occleve and Lydgate imitated, as closely as their
talents would allow, the rhythm and metre of their
master, but with far different results ; indeed, it
often seems as if these latter rhymesters were com-
posing in a foreign tongue, so false is the accent
they impose even when their metre is technically
correct. The French terminations and inflections
which Chaucer so largely used, in the time of Lydgate had become antiquated and inconvenient ; so
he, and Occleve also, were constrained to apologise
for the obvious roughness of their lines :

" And trouthe of metre I sette also a-syde;
    For of that art I hadde as tho no guyde
    Me to reduce, whan I went a-wronge :
    I toke none hede nouther of shorte nor longe."

This is the simple truth ; a foot more or less was
absolutely of no importance to such a literary cen-
tipede as Dan John Lydgate : yet to him, and in a
far less degree to Occleve, we of to-day owe a debt
of gratitude.

If it had not been for the effort of such minor
poets, vernacular literature would have been choked

amid the obstacles which blocked its path. In early times the authors of repute who composed serious works, rejecting the crude and imperfect vehicle of the English tongue, wrote for men as learned as themselves, and almost invariably clothed their ideas in the classic cadence of the Latin language, at that time the universal medium for all scholars and literary disposed persons.

If such men as Occleve, Lydgate, Hawes, Skelton, and Barclay had not carried on the continuity of English literature, a great blow would have been given not only to letters, but to education in this country. The garden of England in those days was but a semi-cultured waste, overgrown with forest and tangled underwood, depressed with foggy fen and vapid marsh; as it was with the land, so it was with the literature. To us, with all the advantages and improvements of the nineteenth century, the compositions of these early writers seem to bristle with absurdities, and abound in platitudes; but a sympathetic eye can see that when the pools were drained, and the thorns, by more skilful gardeners, were budded with poetic roses, in the full time the blossoms gave to the world of literature many a garland of fair and fragrant flowers. I feel, indeed, in occupying the attention of a society of eminence, in these days of rapid progress, with such old and obsolete writers, that I run the risk of being accused of inconsequence; but my excuse must be that, as the English nation spreads and increases, every circumstance, no matter how trivial, is of importance which tells us something of the building up of that great English

language and literature which has been the means
of giving to the human race some of the noblest
conceptions in which the mind of man has been
permitted to reflect the wisdom of God.

"THE PASTON LETTERS," WITH SPECIAL REFERENCE TO THE SOCIAL LIFE OF THE FOURTEENTH AND FIFTEENTH CENTURIES.

BY SAMUEL DAVEY, F.R.S.L.

THE unique collection of the records of a past age, commonly known as " The Paston Letters," consists of about 1000 original letters and documents, written during the reigns of Henry V, Henry VI, Edward IV, Richard III, and Henry VII by certain members of the Paston family and various persons of note and consequence, the whole extending over a period from 1417—19 to 1509. The earliest epistles are from William Paston, known as the good judge, who was born in 1378, and from Agnes, his wife. This same Judge Paston, who is mentioned in 'Fuller's Worthies,' bought an estate from the son of the poet Chaucer. A great number of these letters were written either by or to John Paston, of the Inner Temple, the son of the judge aforesaid, and his wife, Margaret Paston; also Sir John Paston, their eldest son, his younger brother, likewise named John, and many other members of the family. There are letters also from most of the royal and eminent personages of the realm including King Henry VI, Edward IV, Henry VII, Thomas Bourchier, Archbishop of Canterbury, George Nevill, Archbishop of York, John Mowbray and John Howard, Dukes of Norfolk, Richard Earl of Warwick, Richard Duke of York, William and John Dukes of Suffolk, John de Vere, Earl of Oxford, Lord Hastings, Richard Earl of Salisbury, Humphrey Duke of Buckingham, Lord Cromwell, Sir John Fastolf, and many others.

Of the historical value of the Paston Letters, Mr. Hallam, referring to an imperfect edition, says that they "are an important testimony to the progressive condition of society, and come in as a precious link in the chain of moral history of England, which they alone in this period supply. They are unique, so far as I know, in Europe; for, though it is highly probable that in the archives of Italian families, if not in France or Germany, a series of merely private letters, equally ancient, may be concealed, I do not recollect that any have been published. They are all written in the reigns of Henry VI and Edward IV (except a few that extend as far as Henry VII) by different members of a wealthy and respectable, but not noble family, and are therefore pictures of the English gentry of that age. It is plain that several members of the family, male and female, wrote not only grammatically, but with fluency and facility and epistolary expertness, which imply the habitual use of the pen." Another valuable testimony concerning these letters was from Horace Walpole, an eminent letter-writer himself, who said, "The letters of Henry VI's time have come out, and to me make all other letters not worth reading. I have gone through one volume, and cannot bear to be writing when I am so eager to be reading." Some account of these letters may not be out of place in the

Chaucer celebration of 1900, as they reveal more than any other contemporary records the social state of England about the time when our great poet lived and flourished. History is marked more by epochs than by centuries, for " as in to-day already walks to-morrow," so the fourteenth century carried its ecclesiastical, legal, and civil procedure into the fifteenth, with its coincidences of institutions, customs, and manners, thus making a continuity which was not broken until the Wars of the Roses. Through the Paston Letters we see how well Chaucer has depicted the characters of his own age. In the Prologue to the ' Canterbury Tales ' the poet shows himself at home also with all mankind, and as long " as the same heart beats in every breast " he will claim kindred with future generations.

The following among the notable personages who figure in the Paston correspondence were living in Chaucer's time : Cardinal Beaufort, Sir William de la Pole, Duke of Suffolk, Richard Beauchamp, Earl of Warwick, John Duke of Bedford, Sir John Fortescue, Humphrey Duke of Gloucester, Sir John Fastolf. Many of the early writers of the Paston Letters were contemporaries of the poet; and nearly all the characters described in the Prologue—the Knight, the Squire, the Yeoman, the Monk, the Friar, the Clerk, the Franklin, the Poor Parson, &c.—are alive in this correspondence just as Chaucer saw them,—not on pilgrimage in the pleasing hyperbole of poetic fiction, but in active life going about their daily concerns, and in their usual habit and dress. It would be impossible in our limited

time and space to make an abstract of these 1000
letters and documents, neither would it serve our
purpose to do so, seeing how large a portion of
their contents has become obsolete, and very difficult to understand; especially is it so in the old
legal documents, charters and cartularies, through
the decrepit vocabulary of archaic forms relating
to people long dead and forgotten. Much, however, there is to be made new, and many an old dry
bone has to go through "a sort of Medea-like process" in order to come out in its pristine freshness
so as to resuscitate the past. Though the habits
of the English people remained with little change
during the fourteenth to the middle of the fifteenth
century, yet soon after Chaucer's death their language gradually underwent a considerable alteration,
and a great number of French and Saxon words were
eliminated from it. This change is noticeable even
in the earliest, but more especially in the latest of
the Paston Letters, where, no doubt, the language
relating to the common affairs of life was written as
it was spoken by the people; and it is not very
difficult, even in the unsettled orthography of the
time, to read and understand the words of every-day
use. But it must be borne in mind that the literary
language gradually refined and partly transformed
the colloquial, with its various dialects. We shall
endeavour to present from these old, dry, and faded
letters and worm-eaten chronicles, taken out of the
dusty lumber-room of time, a faithful and authentic
picture of the social and domestic life of the people;
the manners, customs, amusements, general humour,
and condition of the England that *was*, such as we

cannot get from any set history, or hardly from any other source. Although so many private letters were written by and to the Paston family during the struggle between the houses of York and Lancaster, it is only occasionally that references are made to the bloody battles of that period. Thus the chief interest of the correspondence relates to the social and every-day life of the time. When kings were being imprisoned, dethroned, or killed, and princes murdered, when the rival parties during these conflicts were settling their differences, like the Queen of Hearts in 'Alice in Wonderland,' by "chopping off heads," the farmer was sowing his seed as usual, or watching his corn ripen, quaffing his ale, or discussing the agricultural prospects with his neighbours—so little effect did these rival contests appear to have produced on the social and domestic life of our ancestors. But intermixed with the Paston correspondence are a number of miscellaneous letters and State papers relating to the chief historical events of these troublous times, which must have come into the possession of the family through some indirect channel. There is a curious account of the Commons of Kent under Jack Cade in 1450, written by an eye-witness who was taken prisoner by the rebels and condemned to death, but afterwards escaped. There are letters written also by some of the principal men of the Yorkist and Lancastrian parties, who were witnesses of nearly all the battles which they describe. Most of the members of the Paston family were engaged in these conflicts. Sir John Paston and his brother were both at the battle of Barnet, where the former was

wounded. These historical letters can only incident-
ally be referred to, as our main purpose is to show,
from the earlier and more important part of the
Paston correspondence, that the social manners and
customs of the English people, both in town and
country, had hardly changed from the period of
Chaucer to the Wars of the Roses.

We read how the men of this remote time lived,
loved, worshipped, fought, went to law, and finally
made their wills and died. There is a strange and
almost wild pathos of resignation about some of
their deaths; for with all their stubborn tenacity of
life, they quailed not before the arch foe, but as
calmly laid their heads upon the block as upon the
pillow, or made the battle-field their bed; and in the
words of a contemporary,

> " They willingly gave themselves to the gentle and dear
> and much-desired embraces of our mother earth;"

feeling, no doubt, with the poet, that—

> " Ease after toyle, port after stormy seas,
>   Peace after war, death after life, doth greatly please."

Nor did they dwell upon their griefs with morbid
persistence. What Tacitus wrote about their fore-
fathers was also true of them :

> "They got done with their weeping quickly, but they
> keep their sorrows long."

These people dwelt oftentimes remote from towns,
and news came slowly,—not minute by minute from
all parts of the world, as in the present day. Nor

was the air full of words, for they knew very little
of that multitudinous personage called the Public.
They talked with their pens more about their domestic concerns—the wooings and marriages of
their sons and daughters, and their bringing up in
the world. We read of the old and ever youthful
episodes of love, which brighten the commonplace
sequence of every-day existence; of the various
interests and affairs of State and station, which
relieve the monotony of what is called "high life."
And it is remarkable that through all their troubles
and distresses—and they had many—except in one
or two instances, there is scarcely a murmur or
complaint about "the wretchedness of the world."
And no trace is to be found of that desponding,
sneering scepticism which is characteristic of some
of our modern pessimists. One of the writers,
during the worst troubles of the time, expresses
herself in a very philosophical manner: "It is a
strange world, God amend it when He will." These
men were evidently able, in the words of Martial,—

> "To look on life with placid eye,
> And never fear or wish to die."

A few scarred and grey veterans after fighting their
battles, retired from the world and purchased a re-
treat in some religious house. They choose—

> "The castle for their stormy life,
> The convent for its close."

In a letter addressed to John Paston from one of
his relatives, when the former was going through a

series of troubles and misfortunes, the writer gives
the following advice :—" And how that ever ye do,
hold up your manship." These quaint words re-
mind us of Thackeray's noble lines :

" Come wealth or want, come good or ill,
    Let young and old accept their part,
And bow before the awful will,
    And bear it with an honest heart.
Who misses, or who wins the prize,
    Go, lose, or conquer as you can ;
But if you fail, or if you rise,
    Be each, pray God, a gentleman ! "

The country gentlemen of the period we are
describing were, in times of peace, mostly engaged
in hunting, hawking, and fishing. They were
taught to ride, to shoot, and above all things to
speak the truth ; thoroughly English in blood,
bone, and brain, fond of litigation and of asserting
their rights, though sometimes not over-scrupulous
in enforcing them. They evidently believed—

" In the good old plan
That they should take who had the power,
    And they should keep who can."

The passion for getting and keeping land was
intense among the better classes, and the life of the
Pastons, male and female, was one long game of
law for the possession and retention of their property and estates. These men were strong in their
passions, in their virtues, and their vices ; haters
in the main of double-dealing. If a man is a villain
he speaks and acts as such, as if he was fully aware

that others knew it as well as himself ; and now
and then we come across one of Chaucer's " stick-
at-nothing " villains—" The smiler with the knife
, hid under the cloak." The maxim of one of the
Greek philosophers that " Love and Hate govern
the world " may be well illustrated in the strong
and direct impulsive life of these men. The women
were generally loving and obedient—

> " Faithful, true, and kind,
> Without offence of mutabilitie."

Yet they had not that invertebrate amiability which
Pope satirised as " No character at all." They
might have been included in Chaucer's ' World of
Ladies,' for his patient Grisilde, Constance, Margaret, Emilie, and others, were not mere fictions
any more than Mrs. Bailly, the shrewish wife of
the host of the Tabard, or that jolly, rosy vixen, the
wife of Bath, who had had five husbands, one of
whom she boasted—

> " That in his owen grease I made him frie
> For anger, and for veray jealousie."

The women represented in the Paston Letters
are not ideal characters, though some of them
would quite realise Chaucer's conception of what a
good woman should be. Chaucer, like Shakespeare, had a noble idea of womanhood. To his
mind a good woman was a compendium of all
human excellence. He does not make her an angel,
but a " dearer being." He painted his women
nearer perfection than his men, for he says—

"There can no man in humbleness him acquite
As woman can, nor be half so true as woman be."

There were episodes in the lives of the Paston
family, male and female, which might form materials
for half a dozen romances. Some of the women
who played a part in that evolving human drama
were made of the same stuff as Chaucer's heroines.

The men and women in these letters are clearly
seen, real, distinct, and complete, endeavouring to
do their duty, sometimes in their own rough way,
but according to the lights they had. It was not
always a word and a blow, for often the blow came
first. We read of mothers who thought that there
were more things to be dreaded in their sons than
death, "Who would rather they were buried than
lost for default." Nor was it an effeminate age,
although the young men wore bonnets and gowns.
They were of "the good yeomen whose limbs were
made in England." Nevertheless, it was rather a
rough time for youth; parental authority was strict,
and the *argumentum baculinum* was much relied on.
In one of the articles under which the Earl of
Warwick took charge of the person of the young
king, Henry VI, in 1432, there was a proviso that
he had power to chastise his royal pupil for his
"defaults or trespasses." Agnes Paston writes to
her son's tutor in London, and prays him, "if he
hath not done well, or will not amend, to belash
him till he will amend, as did the last master, the
best he ever had at Cambridge." She evidently
believed in the Arabian proverb that "The stick
came down from heaven." This same Agnes

Paston was one of the most mercenary of match-
makers, but she found that the heart was a dreadful
impediment to the making of a bargain, when there
was some reciprocal entanglement between two
lives, each of which refused to be sold, or "to
choose love by another's eyes." As one instance
out of many of the barbarous treatment inflicted
by parents upon their children, it is related of this
said Agnes Paston that when her daughter Elizabeth
was sought in marriage by Stephen Scrope, a
widower of about fifty years of age, at first both
mother and daughter were not averse to the match,
"if it be that his land stand clear." For some un-
explained reason, but probably because his land
did not stand clear, the mother made an objection
to the marriage; and as the daughter was not
willing to give up her lover, she was imprisoned in
the house, constantly watched, and subjected to
such cruel treatment that a relative wrote to John
Paston to interfere on behalf of his sister, saying
that "She was never in so great sorrow as she is
now-a-days; for she has, since Easter, the most
part been beaten once in the week or twice, and
sometimes twice a day; and her head broken in two
or three places." This marriage, as might be expected, never came off, for Elizabeth Paston, with
her mother's consent (as no doubt the land stood
clear), was afterwards happily married to Robert
Poynings, a connection of the Duke of Northumber-
land, and again to Sir George Browne. It was said
by Balzac that "life would hardly be possible without a great deal of forgetting;" so evidently
thought Elizabeth Paston, for in spite of the brutal

treatment she had received, she wrote afterwards the most affectionate letters addressed to " My right worshipful and most entirely beloved mother."

Many of the peculiar laws, customs, and traditions of this time relating to marriage are described. In nearly all the wooings there were constant bickerings between the parents of both families, for marriages were generally arranged by parents and guardians, and there was a great deal of higgling in the matrimonial market, especially to know if " the land stood clear." Marriage was evidently looked upon as a reciprocity of interests. We see this in the account given of the vagrant amours of John Paston the younger, the son of Margaret Paston. This gentleman's adventures and misadventures in search of a wife are very amusing. He is constantly writing to his mother and his brother, Sir John Paston, or to any one who could render him assistance, urging them to find for him a first-rate investment for his affections in cash or land, or, in other words, a wife with a fortune. He proposed to more than a dozen ladies, and sometimes he had two or three matrimonial engagements on hand at the same time, no matter whether the lady was young or old, of noble or ignoble birth, beautiful or ugly, so long as he could annex her fortune. Money he wanted and money he must have, for money was everything and all things to him. After a great deal of bargaining, in which he endeavoured to levy blackmail on both sides of the family, an agreement was signed for a marriage. The choice he made was a good one, as the lady was devotedly attached to him. Before her marriage she wrote two simple and artless love-letters and a valentine. Some extracts from these may be interesting as a specimen of love epistles, written more than four hundred years ago. Poor lady, the bargaining about her goods (fortune) was going on at this time. She begins :—

" Right reverend and worshipful, and my right well-beloved valentine, I recommend me unto you, full heartily desiring to hear of your welfare, which I beseech Almighty God long for to preserve unto his pleasure and your heart's desire. And, if it please you to hear of my welfare, I am not in good health of body nor of heart, nor shall be till I hear from you. . . . And my lady my mother hath laboured the matter to my father full diligently, but she can no more get than ye know of (she refers to her dower), for the which God knoweth I am full sorry. But if that ye love me, as I trust verily that ye do, ye will not leave me therefore : for if that ye had not half the livelihood (income) that ye have, for to do the greatest labour that any woman alive might I would not forsake you."

In another letter she says :—

" Wherefore, if that ye could be content with that good (goods) and my poor person I would be the merriest maiden on ground ; and if ye think not yourself so satisfied, or that ye might have much more good (goods) as I have understood by you afore, good, true, and loving valentine, that ye take no such labour upon you as to come more for that matter, but let (what) is pass and never more to be spoken of, as I may be your true lover and beads-woman* during my life."

Of all love-letters, we know of none more tender

* A beadsman or beadswoman, one who prays for another.

or more touching than these; she is willing to sacrifice herself entirely for his happiness. Like Chaucer's Creseide, she could say—

> " But I with all mine herte and all my might,
>   As I have saied, woll love unto my last
> My owne dear herte, and all mine owne knight."

After her marriage the letters to her husband are full of affection on her side. No doubt John Paston loved his wife, as much as his cold, selfish nature was capable of loving anything besides himself.

At this time a guardian under the feudal dues had a perfect right to sell his ward to a man of property, who could compel him to marry his own son or daughter. We have an instance of this in the case of Stephen Scrope, who was a son-in-law and ward of Sir John Fastolf, and Fastolf cleared 500 marks by selling his wardship to Chief Justice Gascoigne in order to marry him to one of his daughters. Scrope bitterly complains of his guardian, that " he bought and sold him as a beast, against all right and law." This same Stephen Scrope had himself to resort to the same system, for he writes, " For very need I was fain to sell a little daughter I have for much less than I should have done by possibility." This unjust law was repealed in the reign of Charles II.

No wonder, under the harsh and cruel treatment of mercenary parents and guardians, that love should sometimes sicken and decay, and end in awful tragedy. In the mediæval poems and romances, we may often read of men and women dying of a

malady which has eluded the diagnosis of modern
medical science. It is called in a somewhat homely
phrase, " A broken heart."

It was against these mercenary marriages of his
own time that Chaucer poured out so often the vials
of his wrath in verse, for he could not bear that true
love should be outraged. He says :

> " As would God, tho' wretches that despise
> Service of love had eares also long
> As had Midas, ful of covetise,
>   . . . God yeve hem mischaunce
> And every lover in his trouth avaunce."

Yet these mercenary marriages, when once made,
were as a rule held sacred ; for licentiousness was
not to be tolerated. The tender letters of Margaret
Paston addressed to her husband John Paston in
London are genuine love epistles written from " the
red-leaved volume of the heart." They contain also
the gossip of the time—an account of her domestic
grievances, her quarrels with her servants, who
seemed to have at times given much trouble and
caused great mischief in her household. We read
of little tiffs with her relations, her " sorrow for
her husband's displeasure at her simpleness which
is too heavy to endure with." When he is sick in
the Inner Temple she writes naively, that " She
would rather have him at home than a new gown
if it were of scarlet." Here and there are little
wifely hints about new gowns, collars, girdles, and
necklaces, and a tender reproach sometimes that
her dresses are not quite up to date among so many
fresh gentlewomen of the time," but everything is

said in love and not in anger. This Margaret
Paston was no mercenary match-maker. When
there was a chance of her son marrying a near
relation of King Edward IV, she writes to him :

" As ye have the voice in this country, that ye may do
as much with the king as any knight that is belonging to
the court . . . and also that ye should marry right nigh
of the queen's blood, what she is, we are not quite certain,
but if it be so that your land should come again by the
reason of your marriage, and to be set in rest, at the
reverence of God forsake it not, *if ye can find in your
heart to love her,* so that she be such one as ye can think
to have issue by, or else, by troth, I had rather that ye
never married in your life."

It was the custom for the sons of gentlemen to
be sent at an early age to serve in some good
family, and we learn that these gentlemen, attending upon their lords, were obliged to appear dressed
in their livery gowns for the most part every day.
John Paston, the younger, was brought up in the
family of John Mowbray, Duke of Norfolk, and it
was considered a necessary part of a gentleman's
education for his knowledge of the world to be thus
trained. In Shakespeare's time it was said that
" Home keeping youth have ever homely wits."
Young gentlewomen of good family were brought
up also as attendants upon ladies of rank. They
were taught all kinds of needlework, cooking,
making pastry, simple medicaments, &c. We find
Margaret Paston writing to her son, Sir John
Paston, to try and get his sister " with my Lady
Oxford or my Lady Bedford, or else in some other
worshipful place." Elizabeth Paston, after the

cruel treatment received from her mother, lived in the family of Lady Pole, where she was employed in needlework and to help in various ways, her mother having to pay for her board. This paying for board and boarding out seems to have been a common practice in those days. One of the suitors for the hand of the same Elizabeth Paston when proposing marriage, among the favours to be granted to her was one " that he would not charge her mother for board after the day of the marriage." This marriage never took place. It might have been a happy one, even with the mercenary Agnes Paston for a mother-in-law, if the custom had prevailed as in some remote countries, where, according to Sir John Lubbock, a husband is absolutely forbidden to speak to his mother-in-law.

Another curious custom is mentioned. Margaret Paston, writing to her husband in 1464, says : " The Mayor and Mayoress sent hither their dinners this day, and they dined here. I am beholden to them, for they have sent to me divers times since ye went hence." It was customary after dinner for all classes to have what was called " their sleeping time," like the Roman siesta. This was so universal that it extended even to labourers, who were allowed an hour and a half for dinner and mid-day sleep, from May to August. As this practice was very much abused, an Act of Parliament was afterwards passed to restrict it.

It is chiefly through this correspondence that we learn the state of education in the fifteenth century. The letters written to the Paston family were from " all sorts and conditions of men "—from friends,

neighbours, noblemen, stewards, and domestic
servants; they all could write. If Charles Lamb's
friend Norris complained that "he found much indifferent spelling in Chaucer," he would certainly
have been bewildered by the cacography of some
of these letters. During the persecutions of the
Lollards, the ability of the humbler classes to read
and write English was shown in the depositions of
various witnesses and informers at the trials of some
of the members of this religious society in 1429.
It is difficult to account for the spread of education
among the people. The clergy on whom devolved
the duty of instructing the young were, as a rule,
very illiterate, and many of them were aliens. This
was the case in Chaucer's time, when Edward III
remonstrated with the Pope for bestowing rich bene-
fices, &c., "upon unqualified mercenary foreigners
who could not even understand the language."
Nor were the native clergy at this period much
better instructed. At an entertainment given in
Rome to the Pope and Cardinals by Andrew Forman,
Bishop of Murray, and papal legate for Scotland,
that dignitary blundered so in his Latinity when he
said grace that his holiness and the cardinals tittered,
and the bishop testily concluded the blessing by
giving, "All the false carles to the de'il." The
company, misunderstanding the malediction, devoutly said, Amen.

A genuine specimen occurs in this correspondence of an Eton schoolboy's letter, from which it is
manifest that the natural vigour of the writer's
mental faculties had not been impaired by over-
study. Referring to this curious epistle, Mr. Hallam

says, "a letter from Master William Paston at Eton proves that Latin versification was taught there, as early as the beginning of Edward IV's reign. It is true that the specimen he rather proudly exhibits does not much differ from what we denominate nonsense verses, but a more material observation is that the sons of country gentlemen living at a considerable distance were already sent to public schools for grammatical education."

There is an account of Walter Paston's expenses at Oxford in the year 1478; and we may fairly estimate the cost of his university education at about £100 a year in our present money. At this time the University had greatly decreased in the number of its scholars, which scarcely amounted to 6,000. In the year 1357 (during Chaucer's time) the Archbishop of Armagh, Richard Fitz-Ralph, in his evidence before the consistory at Avignon, stated that there had been as many as 30,000 scholars in his day. This estimate may be an exaggeration, for Anthony Wood, in his ' History and Antiquities of Oxford,' says : " But among these a company of varlets who pretended to be scholars, shuffled them-selves in and did act much villany in the university, by thieving, loose living, quarrelling, &c." The mediæval undergraduate students were mainly lads of humble origin. Even villeins sent their sons to go through an Oxford course, and these poor scholars supported themselves during term by manual labour or from charity, which may account for the proletarian clergy of the Middle Ages.

In the Paston Letters pilgrimages to various shrines are mentioned as of frequent occurrence.

These, with their motley sights of shows and processions, must have given, as in Chaucer's time, a certain objective picturesqueness and variety to the out-door life of the people, both in town and country, for kings, queens, princes, noblemen—indeed men and women of every degree made pilgrimages to the different shrines throughout the country.

In one of the early Paston Letters a learned judge is represented as ascribing all his good fortune to his visits to our Lady's house at Walsingham. Margaret Paston writes to her husband, during his illness in London, " My mother behested (vowed) another image of wax of the weight of you, to our Lady of Walsingham, and she sent four nobles (£1 6s. 8d.) to the four orders of friars at Norwich to pray for you, and I have behested to go on pilgrimage to Walsingham, and to St. Leonard's (Norwich) for you." It was this celebrated shrine of our Lady at Walsingham that Erasmus not long afterwards visited, and gave such a graphic description in one of his ' Colloquies,' " Peregrinatio religionis ergo." We learn that young ladies visited shrines in order to pray for good husbands; perhaps they might have asked for something worse. John Paston the younger advises his mother, when in London, " among other things, to visit the Rood of North door (a cross beside St. Paul's) and St. Saviour's at Bermondsay, and let my sister Margary go with you to pray to them that she may have a good husband ere she come home again."

There is nothing more significant of the character of a people than how they take their pleasures. What are their recreations, their holy-day diversions

—the sports and amusements which are evolved out of their national life? In the fourteenth and fifteenth centuries, amongst all classes there was a fondness for out-door pastimes and athletic sports ; also for the acting of stage plays, the witnessing of comical shows and spectacles, pageants and mysteries, in which music played an important part, with the various accompaniments of harps, horns, flutes, pipes, and songs. In the Prologue to the ' Canterbury Tales,' the young squire is described as " singing and fluting all the day." The Friar could sing, and play upon the harp, and while playing his eyes " shone like stars in a frosty night." Even the drunken miller—

> " A baggpipe wel coulde he blowe and soune,
> And therwithall he brought us out of toune."

While Madame Eglentine, the Prioresse—

> " Ful wel she sange the service devine
> Entuned in hire nose ful swetely."

The pilgrims beguiled part of their time in singing love songs, convivial songs, and " songs that shouldn't be sung."

In the Paston Letters there is a record of the same hilarity and cheerfulness in the social life of the people. We read of " the harping, the luting, the singing, and the disguising, the playing at tables, chess and cards." It was a very merry, dancing, laughing, and unthinking time, quite worthy the traditions of " merrie England." Yet with all their hilarity, their love of mirth and fun,

the men and women of that day were not without
strong religious feelings, "for most part of the
silent sort." They were as simple as children, yet
not *childish* in their religious belief, in spite of a
tincture of superstition, or what Matthew Arnold
calls "aberglaube" (over-faith), which, perhaps,
gave a piquancy to their everyday life. They had
light enough to lead them along a straight road.
At this time science was but little known. What
went by the name dealt in astrology, magic, and
sorcery, which would now be regarded as useless
knowledge. There were philosophic sciolists and
learned schoolmen who discussed quodlibets and
talked grave nonsense upon subjects beyond the
reach of human understanding. We are not surprised, then, that there should have been a certain
amount of superstition, not only among the lower,
but also the better classes, for, says Bacon, "In
all superstitions, wise men follow fools." Yet
there is no evidence in these letters that the people
were under the slavish dominion of the priesthood
in spiritual matters. We read very little about the
clergy except when they interfered, as they often
did, in secular affairs; for priests sometimes took
part in popular tumults. In the reign of Henry VI
two bishops were murdered by the populace. Neither
were the priests, or parsons, as they were generally
called, held in any special reverence for their sacred
calling, either in or out of the church. It is related
of a sheriff arresting a person during mass, and the
priest and some of the congregation, after a free
fight, rescuing him; of the bailiff of Eye and the
bailiff of Stradbrook, acting as agents for the Duke

of Suffolk, despoiling a church at Hellesden, near
Norwich, "and bearing away all the goods that were
left there. They stood upon the high altar and
ransacked the images, and took away such as they
might find, and put away the parson out of the
church till they had done." There is an account
also of putting a parson and four of his men in the
stocks on the charge of murder. In another place
it is stated that a subpœna was served on a person
on Trinity Sunday publicly in church. In a letter,
dated 1450, of Sir John Fastolf, addressed to his
agent, Sir Thomas Howys, also a parson, he charges
"Sir John Buck, parson of Stratford, of having
fished his tanks at Dedham, and helped to break
his dam, and destroyed his new mill, ... and
that he and John Cole hath by force this year and
other years taken out of my waters at Dedham to
the number of twenty-four swans and cygnets."
There is an instance of Sir John Fastolf suing the
prior of a convent in a secular court for a rent
charge. After Sir John Fastolf's death, there were
some arrears due to the Abbot of Langley. This
dignitary hints that, until the church dues were paid,
" Sir John Fastolf's soul was in great danger." Of
religious persecutions and the punishment of here-
tics there is nothing told in these letters, although
in the year 1430 a number of Lollards were burnt.
The sufferers were chiefly from the Eastern Counties,
not far from where the Pastons lived. No doubt at
this time the Church was notoriously corrupt, but
there was a remant of good which saved it from
destruction. Chaucer has given his unstudied testimony as to the state of the Church during his time.

Can one forget his full-length portrait of a monk who was "fat as a whale, and walk'd like a swan?" This picture needs no comment, for it tells its own tale. He has also given graphic sketches of the mendicant friar and the Pardoner; of the latter he says—

> "His wallet lay before him in his lappe,
> Bret-ful of pardon come from Rome all hote."

Yet side by side with this motley group, riding, talking, and eating together, are to be found the scholarly clerk of Oxford, who "looked hollow," and the poor parson, the most perfect ideal of a Christian minister to be found in our literature, and which, no doubt, grew out of a reality. As we read some of these Paston Letters, full of reverence and faith, showing us the deep, silent worship of the living soul, we are reminded of the character of "The Plowman," the brother of the Poor Parson in the 'Canterbury Tales,' whose religion was more a life than a creed; for—

> "A good man was he,
> Living in peace and perfect charity,
> God loved he best with his whole heart,
> At alle times . . . .
> And his neighbour right as himselve."

The Paston Letters fully confirm the fidelity of Chaucer's clerical portraits.

As showing the highest expression of the religious feeling of the time, we may refer to the Duke of Suffolk's letter to his son, written just after the sentence of banishment for five years was passed upon him, and a few days before his murder. This composition may take rank as one of the most beautiful letters in our language, and it might have been written by one of the most cultivated minds of the present century. This letter is only known to us through a copy preserved among the Paston Papers. It is addressed to " My dear and only well-beloved Son "—

" I beseech our Lord in Heaven, the Maker of all the world, to bless you, and to send you ever grace to love Him, and to dread Him, to the which, as far as a father may charge his child, I both charge you, and pray you to set all your spirits and wits to do, and to know His holy laws and commandments, by the which ye shall, with His great mercy, pass all the great tempests and troubles of this wretched world.

" And that also, weetingly, ye do nothing for love nor dread of any earthly creature that should displease him. And there as (whenever) any frailty maketh you to fall, beseech His mercy soon to call you to Him again with repentance, satisfaction, and contrition of your heart, never more in will to offend Him.

" Secondly, next Him, above all earthly things, to be true liegeman in heart, in will, in thought, in deed, unto the King aldermost (greatest) high and dread sovereign lord, to whom both ye and I be so much bound to; charging you as father can and may, rather to die than to be the contrary, or to know anything that were against the welfare or prosperity of his most royal person, but that as far as your body and life may stretch ye live and die to defend it, and to let his highness have knowledge thereof in all the haste ye can. Thirdly, in the same wise, I charge you, my dear son, alway as ye be bounden by the commandment of God to do, to love, to worship, your lady and mother; and also that ye obey alway her commandments, and to believe her counsels and advices in all your works, the which dread not, but shall be best and truest to you. And if any other body would steer you to the contrary, to flee the counsel in any wise, for ye shall find it naught and evil.

"Furthermore, as far as father may and can, I charge you in any wise to flee the company and counsel of proud men, of covetous men, and of flattering men the more especially, and mightily to withstand them, and not to draw nor to meddle with them, with all your might and power; and to draw to you and to your company good and virtuous men, and such as be of good conversation, and of truth, and by them shall ye never be deceived nor repent you of. Moreover, never follow your own wit in no wise, but in all your works, of such folks as I write of above, ask your advice and counsel, and doing thus, with the mercy of God, ye shall do right well, and live in right much worship, and great heart's rest and ease. And I will be to you as good lord and father as my heart can think.

"And last of all, as heartily and as lovingly as ever father blessed his child in earth, I give you the blessing of Our Lord and of me, which of His infinite mercy increase you in all virtue and good living; and that your blood may by His grace from kindred to kindred multiply in this earth to His service, in such wise as after the departing from this wretched world here, ye and they may glorify Him eternally, amongst his angels in heaven.

"Written of mine hand
"The day of my departing from this land,
"Your true and loving father,
"April,   "SUFFOLK.
"1450, 28 H. vi."

The next letter in this series, written by Margaret Paston, gives a full and circumstantial account of the Duke of Suffolk's murder at sea, written on the 5th May, 1450.

In the Paston Letters books are rarely mentioned.

Except in a library catalogue Chaucer is not named, nor are his poems, or those of his contemporaries quoted. Books were scarce and expensive. There is an account of the prices paid to William Ebesham for copying books; he charged twopence for writing a folio leaf, three of which he could finish off in a day. A charge is also made of twelve shillings for binding a book, which appears a very high price even for the time. In 1468 we are informed that a copy of the Bible was sold for five marks (more than six guineas of our present money). This must have been a manuscript copy, as there was only one printed edition of the Bible, which would have been more expensive. In 1474 a priest's library, belonging to Sir James Gloys, was sold for twenty shillings and sixpence, or about ten pounds present value. There is part of a catalogue given of the contents of, probably, Sir John Paston's library, which contained 'A book in preente off "The Playe off Chess"' (from the Caxton press). The rest are manuscripts. The catalogue is unfortunately very imperfect. It is written upon a strip of paper about seventeen inches long, and has been rolled up, so that the names of some of the books have been nearly obliterated. Some of the contents are as follows:—' The Death of Arthur,' ' The Story of Guy, Earl of Warwick,' ' King Richard Cœur de Lyon,' ' A Chronicle to Edward III,' Chaucer's ' Troilus and Cressida,' ' The Legend of Good Ladies,' ' The Parliament of Birds,' ' The Temple of Glass,' Bishop Alcock's ' Abbey of the Holy Ghost,' ' The Life of Saint Chrystopher,' ballad of ' Guy and Colbrond,' &c.

There are a number of books on heraldry, on jousts, tournaments, fighting in lists, statutes of war, a book of new statutes from Edward IV, and many others, the titles of which it is impossible to decipher.

There are frequent complaints made in these letters of the earth hunger of the landlords. Even land-grabbers were not unknown, and there were interminable litigations and disputes about the rights of way between the peasants and their lords. The value of land is mentioned as fourpence an acre yearly rent. On the whole the people were prosperous; no mention is made of poverty among the lower classes. The prices paid according to statute during the fourteenth century until the year 1495, when the statutory wages were raised, for a bailiff, £1 4s. 4d. per annum with meat and drink; for a common servant in husbandry when food was found, 15s., and 3s. 4d. for clothes. After the pestilence, from the scarcity of labourers, the statutory wages were held in abeyance. The ordinary wages of an artizan were fourpence per day without food and drink. One penny commanded as much of the necessaries of life as about 1s. 3d. of our present money. According to the 'Liber Albus,' any one overpaying a workman is to be fined forty pence; and the workman taking more than is due, is to be imprisoned for forty days. From the same authority we learn that the prices of nearly everything were regulated by statute, especially articles of wearing apparel, even to boots, shoes, and gloves. Every one was supposed to dress according to his class; but "merchants and others down to people of handicraft, might, if they had property worth five hundred pounds, dress like esquires. There were many laws made at divers times to restrict extravagance in female dress, but as fashion rules the world, there was much indifference on the part of the ladies to these edicts, for they well knew that no civil laws could set aside the absolute supremacy of fashion. Sir John Fortescue, who was Chief Justice of England and Lord Chancellor to Henry VI, when in exile with Queen Margaret and her son (between the years 1463 and 1471) wrote his famous treatise ' De Laudibus Legum Angliæ,' in which he gives a glowing account of the prosperity of this country during the fourteenth and part of the fifteenth century. In contrasting the state of France with that of England, he says, " Every inhabitant of the realm of England useth and enjoyeth at his pleasure all the fruits that his land or cattle beareth, with all the profits and commodities which by his own travail or by the labour of others he gaineth. . . . Hereby it comes to pass that the men are rich, having abundance of gold and silver, and all things necessary for the maintenance of man's life. . . . They eat plentifully of all kinds of flesh and fish. They wear fine woollen cloth in all their apparel. . . . They have great stores of household furnishings and implements of husbandry. . . . Neither are they sued in the law, but only before ordinary Judges," and he adds, " It hath never been known that any of them (the Judges) hath been corrupt with gifts or bribes."

The Paston Letters give a very different account, even before the Wars of the Roses, of the security

of property, and of the impartiality of the judges
as related by Sir John Fortescue. There are many
instances given of noblemen taking possession of
estates contiguous to their own, and turning out
the owners by force of arms if necessary. If these
noblemen had friends at Court, it was simply
impossible for the real owners to regain possession
by any legal means. At divers times several of the
estates of the Paston family were seized and taken
possession of by force.

Not only at this time were there land thieves, but
water thieves as well. The English Channel was
infested with pirates and robbers; for men took to
piracy at sea, as they did to poaching on land.
These outlaws were known as " Rovers of the Sea."
In Chaucer's time, the Merchant, in ' The Canterbury Tales,' wished the sea were guarded " betwix-
teen Middlebury and Orwell " for the safety of his
goods.

Margaret Paston, writing to her husband in 1440,
says " that there came up eleven hundred Flemings
at Waxham, thereof were taken and killed and
drowned eight hundred "; and again, in 1449, she
writes : " There have been many enemies against
Yarmouth and Cromer, and have done much harm,
and taken many Englishmen and put them in great
distress and heavily ransomed them."

Agnes Paston, writing in 1457, after describing
the pillaging going on near the shore, says : " God
give grace that the sea may be better kept than it
is now, or else it shall be a perilous dwelling by the
sea coast." In 1442, both Sandwich and South-
ampton were burned. The sea-ports were so exposed

to depredations that market towns connected with them were placed inland. The men of Tarring, in Sussex, represented that while attending Broadwater Market " many were taken prisoners and slain, as well as the men as the women, childer, maidens, wifes and dorters."

There is an account of election riots, which differ very little from the same disturbances in our own time; also of scandalous reports and libels being sown broadcast among the electors by the opposite parties. What is remarkable is the account of " a dozen towns in England that choose no burgess to send to Parliament which ought to do it." This was in the year 1472.* One of the qualifications given for a member of Parliament was that he can " say well." The Primrose League had not as yet come into existence, although ladies had some influence at elections, and were rewarded for their services. In a letter written from an election agent to a candidate, he is advised " to purchase a goodly ring price twenty shillings " (about ten pounds in our present money), " or some pretty flower the same price, not under, to be given to Jane Roden, for she has been the most especial labourer in your matter." At this time members of Parliament were paid by their constituents.

We must not omit, in treating of the social condition of the people, to mention the plague, or Black Death, which first appeared in England on the 1st of August, 1348, when Chaucer was a youth. It is estimated, from contemporary records, that this

* This was no doubt because it rested with the sheriff to determine what towns should exercise the franchise.

pestilence carried off nearly one half of the population in about fourteen months. These accounts may be over-estimated, as panics always produce exaggeration, and there are no reliable statistics to guide us. During the fourteenth and fifteenth centuries England was never free from this pestilence, while typhoid and leprosy were prevalent as well. In 1485 the sweating sickness broke out, of which there were five visitations in this country; and this disease was almost as destructive to human life as the plague. So much did the poor suffer from the Black Death that the "Statute of Labourers" became of no effect, and the wages of the peasants increased to the extent of nearly 50 per cent.

John Paston writes in 1471 ' that the plague had entered every house in Norwich," and again in 1479 he says "that there was sickness in Norwich and in other borough towns, the most universal death I ever knew in England."

According to our present knowledge of the laws of health and of medicine, and also of the sanitary measures to be taken for the prevention of the spread of disease, the wonder to us is not that people died, but that they lived. Ventilation was unknown, and every precaution was taken which human ingenuity could devise to prevent fresh air from entering the houses. No doubt the air was impure and poisonous, especially in the large towns. During the reign of Henry VI, the Parliament had many times to move from Westminster in consequence of the impurity of the atmosphere. Then again the practice of physic was mixed up with astronomy, astrology, and magic. Even Roger Bacon said that " Astronomy was the better part of medicine." The stars guided the courses of men on land as well as on the sea. If a man died suddenly, he was planet stricken. Pestilences, famines, tempests, and earthquakes were attributed to the malign agencies of demons, who worked through witchcraft, magic, and sorcery. These superstitions may in some measure be accounted for from the fact that the physicians in the Middle Ages were generally monks or ecclesiastics. That they were under the control of the Church is shown by the fact that until 1451 they were not allowed to marry.

The Doctor of Physic in the 'Canterbury Tales' was no doubt drawn from life. He is described as well-grounded in astronomy, and that he kept his patients well by observing the stars and giving his medicines at the right time. From the insight which Chaucer has given of his practice, it is probable that more of his patients died from the doctor than from the disease. One of the doctors in the Paston Letters is described as "a right cunning man and gentil." It would seem that London physicians were not held in very great esteem. Margaret Paston, writing to her husband at the Inner Temple, says, " for God's sake beware what medicines ye take of any physicians in London. I shall never trust to them because of your father, and mine uncle." Why she distrusts them, she does not say. In another letter she wisely recommends kitchen physic, " that ye be well dieted of meat and drink, for that is the greatest help that ye may have none to your health ward."

We learn from these letters that ladies made up medicated drinks,—that water of mint or millefoil (*Achillea millefolium*) was recommended for relieving sickness. There were women also among the lower classes who knew the virtues of herbs and prescribed for various diseases. Some of them, from their knowledge of medicinal plants, with their balsams and cordials, may have been more successful in the treatment of disease than the learned doctor, with his classical and traditional medical lore, combined with his knowledge of astronomy and astrology. Some of the remedies prescribed by the best physicians of the Middle Ages, and continued for some time afterwards, are worthy of a place in the curiosities of medicine. One of the specifics mentioned by Margaret Paston, and others, as most in request, for the cure of the pestilence, was treacle. For the cure of sleeplessness, it was recommended by a celebrated physician, Jerome Cardan, "to anoint the soles of the feet with the fat of a dormouse, the teeth with the ear wax of a dog." For the relief of melancholy a once famous doctor * advised "To bore the skull in two or three places, for that it much avails to the exhalation of the vapours. One of the Court doctors under Edward II, John of Gaddesden (mentioned by Chaucer), in his treatise, 'Rosa Anglica,' gives the following prescription which he had successfully used for the cure of stone :—I collected a good quantity of those beetles which in summer are found

* Salvianus.

in the dung of oxen, also of the crickets which sing
in the fields. I cut off the heads and the wings of
the crickets and put them with the beetles and
common oil into a pot; I covered it and left it
afterwards for a day and night in a bread-oven. I
drew out the pot and heated it at a moderate fire. I
pounded the whole and rubbed the sick parts; in
three days the pain had disappeared." This same
sapient doctor recommended "seven heads of fat
bats" as a remedy for diseases of the spleen. Some
surgeons, when they bled a patient, ordered him to
drink the warm blood so as not to lose the life
which it contained. Other like disgusting practices
were continued down to the seventeenth century,
when the great reformation in medicine took place.
Then there were quacks and mountebanks at nearly
every street corner, and in every village, who had
just wit enough to see through those who could not
see through them. They had their charms, amulets,
philtres, sovereign waters, and absurd nostrums,
the ingredients of which were worthy the contents
of a witches' cauldron, such as dried spiders, sod
earwigs, powdered caterpillars, while human fat
was used as an ointment. Quackery and gullibility
prevailed everywhere, for, says Southey, "man is
a dupeable animal."

Who can wonder that disease in nearly every
form was rampant during the Middle Ages, and
especially the pestilence, or Black Death, which
caused such terrible devastation and destruction of
human life in the fourteenth and fifteenth centuries,
and their ravages continued until science began to
dawn, when men studied the laws of nature, and

humbly strove to understand and obey them? From
that time knowledge has gone on increasing and
widening, and the natural sciences gaining in depth
and breadth; and we can anticipate other and
greater conquests when—

> "This earth,
> Which is the world of all of us, and where
> We find our happiness, or not at all,"

will be made more habitable for us and for coming
generations.

After having followed the chequered fortunes of
the Paston family as related in their long correspondence, our feeling is one of regret that we have
so imperfectly represented them. We have seen
what sort of a world it was which Chaucer must
have looked upon, and some of his contemporaries
have been introduced to us. We have learned how
the Pastons played their part through the various
stages of their history; how they managed their
domestic concerns, and passed their everyday existence. We are impressed also with the thought of
the " broad sameness of the human lot;" that it
alters little as time goes on from age to age.
Though fashions and manners change, the primal
emotions of humanity remain, in spite of circumstances and conditions which can only modify but
cannot transform human nature. "Thus it is,"
says Goethe, "that one people lives, loves, and
feels like another," so that history is ever repeat-
ing itself! These Paston Letters have thrown great
light upon one of the darkest periods of our
social and political history, and their interesting

and varied contents will repay the careful study of
the student, as well as amply reward the intelligent
reader.

AUTHORITIES CONSULTED.

Professor Gairdner's 'Introduction to the Paston Letters,'
3 vols. (Constable).

'Social England.' Edited by H. D. Traill, vol. ii (Cassell).

'Six Centuries of Work and Wages,' Professor J. E. Thorold
Rogers.

ITALIAN INFLUENCE ON CHAUCER.

BY WILLIAM E. A. AXON, F.R.S.L.,

HON. LL.D. WILBERFORCE UNIVERSITY.

AN inquiry into the sources from which Chaucer
drew materials or inspiration receives an additional
justification from the poet's own words. He tells
us in a passage that has become famous,

> " . . . out of oldè feldès, as men seith,
> Cometh al this newè corn from yeer to yere ;
> And out of oldè books, in good feith,
> Cometh al this newè science that men lere." *

A lover of paradox might say that in the Middle
Ages there was no such literary crime as plagiarism.
The "strength of sin is the law," and there was
then no commandment in the literary decalogue
that forbade the use by one author of the facts or
thoughts that he found in the books of another
writer. Where an author is cited it is more frequently for the sake of the authority of a weighty
name than as an acknowledgment of his proprie-
tary rights. Literature was public property where
every one took what seemed good to him, and
expected in turn to be plundered by others.
Chaucer is more scrupulous than some of the
writers of the Middle Ages, and the list of the
authorities whom he cites is a long one. In his

* 'Parlament of Fowles,' 22—25. The quotations are from the
'Globe' edition of Chaucer.

earlier work he is considerably indebted to the French literature of the period, but later he came under Italian influence. Once certainly, and perhaps twice, he visited that country. The relation of our first great modern poet to the mighty mind of Dante, and to Petrarca, and to Boccaccio is a matter of deep interest for the student both of English and Italian literature.

In considering the extent of Chaucer's indebtedness it must be remembered that as there was a considerable body of doctrine and illustration that formed, so to speak, the common stock-in-trade of the literature of the Middle Ages, it is not sufficient to point out resemblances between one author and another, since both may have drawn their inspiration from the same source. Thus the ' Man of Law's Tale' is said by Dunlop to be principally taken from the ' Pecorone' of Ser Giovanni Fiorentino, who began to write his book in 1378, and was therefore a contemporary of Chaucer. There are other Italian versions, including a miracle play by Antonia Pulci. But the ' Man of Law's Tale' is now acknowledged to be in the main taken from Nicholas Trivet's Anglo-French ' Chronicles.' This story of the persecuted wife has been traced by Mr. W. A. Clouston to oriental sources.*

In the ' Monk's Tale' there is an account of Hercules which is taken partly from Boethius,† following closely the poet's own prose translation.

---

* Furnival, Brock, and Clouston. ' Originals and Analogues of some of the Canterbury Tales,' 1872—1867, p. 367.

† The reference in the ' Globe' Chaucer is erroneous; it should be ' De Consolatione,' bk. iv, met. 7.

The remainder is mainly from Ovid. Then comes a statement as to the pillars of Hercules in these two puzzling lines :

> " At bothe the worldè's endès, seith Trophee,
> In stide of boundès he a pileer sette."

What book or author are we to understand by Trophee ? The marginal note on the Ellesmere and Hengwrt MSS., ' Ille vates Chaldeorum Tropheus,' is eminently one of those explanations which do not explain. Dr. Skeat has shown that the mention of the pillars of Hercules comes from Guido Colonna's ' Historia Troiana,' as also some other passages of ' Troilus and Cressida.'* Lydgate tells us that this book was written in the Lombard tongue. There is no satisfactory explanation of the word ' Trophe.' Dr. Skeat suggests that Tropæus may have been the name of the pillars at Terranova which were also called " Columne Hercules " from which Guido's name " delle Colonne " was derived, or that he " may have been connected with Tropia, on the west coast of Calabria, less than fifty miles from Messina, where he was a judge." Mr. W. M. Rossetti thinks it is a form of the word " trophy," in the sense of " love conquered " as a translation of ' Filostrato.' It would appear that we have not yet got the clue to the mystery.

The main Italian influences on Chaucer are those of Dante, Petrarca, and Boccaccio.

There is no reason to doubt that Chaucer was

---

* There is a full discussion of Chaucer's indebtedness to Guido in the 'Complete Works of Geoffrey Chaucer,' edited by the Rev. Walter Skeat, LL.D., Oxford, 1894—1897, vol. ii, p. lv, *et seq.*

well acquainted with Dante's great work. Yet the amount of direct borrowing is not large. There are certain passages as to which there can be no mistake, but they are not numerous. There are others which have been cited in evidence, but which may easily have come from other sources, and as easily have originated in Chaucer's own quick working imagination. When two poets touch upon the same theme it is not necessary to suppose that in all cases the later one has borrowed from his predecessor. Some of the analogies which zealous students have unearthed are far from convincing. Some, indeed, fail ludicrously when tested by the law of evidence. The ' House of Fame' one critic has discovered to be in three books, and he has made the parallel discovery that the ' Divina Commedia' is also in three books. The two facts are incontestable, but, after all, they do not prove anything as to the relations between Dante and Chaucer.*

The passages as to which there is no doubt are sufficient for our purposes.

In the ' Second Nun's Tale' there is an invocation to the Virgin Mary which is taken, in part, from the first twenty-one lines of Canto 33 of the ' Paradiso.' The translation is not very close, and it has even been suggested that both Dante and Chaucer may have taken their ideas from some Latin prayer or hymn.†

---

* This criticism is cited by Prof. T. R. Lounsbury, in his 'Studies in Chaucer' (ii, 239), who mercifully withholds the name of the person who made the great discovery.

† The quotations are from the Oxford ' Dante.'

" Vergine madre, figlia del tuo Figlio,
    Umile ed alta più che creatura,
    Termine fisso d'eterno consiglio,
Tu se' colei che l'umana natura
    Nobilitasti sì, che il suo Fattore
    Non disdegnò di farsi sua fattura.
Nel ventre suo si raccese l'amore,
    Per lo cui caldo nell'eterna pace
    Così è germinato questo fiore.
Qui sei a noi meridiana face
    Di caritate, e giuso intra i mortali
    Sei di speranza fontana vivace.
Donna, sei tanto grande e tanto vali,
    Che qual vuol grazia ed a te non ricorre,
    Sua disianza vuol volar senz' ali.
La tua benignità non pur soccorre
    A chi domanda, ma molte fiate
    Liberamente al domandar precorre.
In te misericordia, in te pietate,
    In te magnificenza, in te s'aduna
    Quantunque in creatura e di bontate."

This hymn has been thus rendered by Longfellow :*

" Thou Virgin Mother, daughter of thy Son,
    Humble and high beyond all other creature,
    The limit fixed of the eternal counsel,
Thou art the one who such nobility
    To human nature gave that its Creator
    Did not disdain to make himself its creature.
Within thy womb rekindled was the love,
    By heat of which in the eternal peace
    After such wise this flower has germinated.
Here unto us thou art a noonday torch
    Of charity, and below there among mortals

* The quotations are from the 'Riverside' edition of Longfellow's Works.

Thou art the living fountain head of hope.
Lady, thou art so great, and so prevailing,
  That he who wishes grace now runs to thee,
  His aspirations without wings would fly.
Not only thy benignity gives succor
  To him who asked it but often times
  Forerunneth of its own accord the asking.
In thee compassion is, in thee, is pity,
  In thee magnificence; in thee unites
  Whate'er of goodness is in any creature."

It is to be noted that Dante places this prayer in the mouth of St. Bernard, and Chaucer follows this ascription in the lines by which he introduces the Invocation to Mary in the 'Second Nun's Tale.'

" And thow that flour of virginès art alle,
  Of whom that Bernard list so well to write;
  To thee at my bigynnyng, first I call,
  Thou confort of us wrecches, do me endite
  Thy maydens deeth, that wan thurgh hir merite,
  The eternal lyf, and of the feend victorie
  As man may after reden in hire storie."

This may possibly indicate that Chaucer regarded Bernard of Clairvaux as the first author of the hymn which he now proceeds to translate from Dante.

" Thow mayde and mooder, doghter of thy sone,
  Thow welle of mercy, synful soulès cure,
  In whom that God, for bountee, chees to wone,
  Thow humble, and heigh over every creature,
  Thow nobledst so ferforth oure nature,
  That no disdeyn the Maker hadde of kynde
  His sone in blood and flessh to clothe and wynde.

Withinne the cloistre blisful of thy sydis
Took mannès shape the eterneel Love and Pees,
That of the trynè compas lord and gyde is,
Whom erthe and see, and hevene, out of relees,
Ay heryen ; and thou virgine wemmèlees.*
Baar of thy body, and dweltest mayden pure,
The creatour of every creature.

Assembled is in thee magnificence,
With mercy, goodnesse, and with swich pitee,
That thou, that art the sonne of excellence,
Nat oonly helpest hem that preyen thee,
But often tyme of thy benygnytee,
Ful frely, er that men thyn help biseche,
Thou goost biforn and art hir lyvès leche."

Possibly, too, the phrase which Chaucer used
later in the same invocation :

"O thou that art so fair and full of grace,
Be myn advócat in that heighè place,
Theras withouten ende is songe Osanne,
Thow Cristès mooder, doghter deere of Anne !"

may be a reminiscence of—

"Di contro a Pietro vedi sedere Anna,
Tanto contenta di mirar sua figlia,
Che non move occhi per cantare *Osanna*." †

Here, as elsewhere, it is to be remarked that
Chaucer treats his material freely, and is no servile
imitator. The 'Second Nun's Tale' is "a comparatively early production," afterwards incorporated in the 'Canterbury Tales.'

Amongst the examples of tragic fortune cited by

* Spotless.
† 'Paradiso,' xxxii, 133.

the Monk is that of Ugolino of Pisa, starved to death
with his children in 1289. This is taken from Canto
32 of the 'Inferno,' but there are some changes.
In Dante the story is necessarily placed in the mouth
of Ugolino, but in Chaucer the narrative is that of
a sympathetic historian.   Dante mentions three
children, Chaucer four, and adds the pathetic touch :

> "The eldeste scarsly fyf yeer was of age.
> Allas ! Fortúne ! it was greet crueltee,
> Swiche briddes for to putte in swich a cage ! "

At the end of the episode Chaucer observes :

> " Whoso wol here it in a lenger wise,
> Redeth the gretè poet of Ytaille
> That hightè Dant, for he kan all devyse
> Fro point to point,—nat o word wol he faille."

Chaucer has, in effect, condensed the ninety-one
lines of Dante into about fifty, which include some
variations, as well as the additional touch already
cited.

A passage from Dante is quoted without much
dramatic propriety by the Wife of Bath.   The hand
may be that of the wanton wife, but the voice is that
of Chaucer :

> "Wel kan the wisè poete of Florence,
> That hightè Dant, speken in this sentence,—
> Lo in swich maner rym is Dantes tale,—
> ' Ful selde upriseth by his branches smale
>   Prowesse of man, for God of his goodnesse
>   Wole that of hym we clayme our gentilesse ;
>   For of our eldrès may we nothing clayme,
>   But temporel thyng that man may hurte and mayme.' "

This is taken from the well-known passage in the ' Purgatorio.'*

> " Rade volte risurge per li rami
> L'umana probitate : e questo vuole
> Quei che la dà, perchè da lui si chiami."

It may not be without interest to compare Longfellow's translation of this sentiment :

> " Not oftentimes upriseth through the branches
> The probity of man ; and this He wills
> Who gives it, so that we may ask of Him."

Dante's fine phrase in the sentence—

> " Lo bel pianeta che ad amar conforta,
> *Facera tutto rider l'oriente,*
> Velando i Pesci ch'erano in sua scorta."

is thus appropriated :

> " And firy Phebus riseth up so brighte
> That al the orient laugheth of the lighte." †

A single phrase of ' Anelida and Arcite '—

> " So thirleth with the poynt of remembrance
> The sword of sorowe, y-whet with fals plesaunce,
> Myn hertè bare of blis, and blak of hewe,"

has, it is thought, been suggested by—

> " Onde lì molto volte se ne piagne
> Per la puntura della rimembranza,
> Che solo ai pii dà delle calcagne." ‡

This is rendered by Longfellow—

> " Whence often we weep for them afresh,
> From pricking of remembrance, which alone
> To the compassionate doth set its spur."

* Canto vii, 121—123.
† ' Purgatorio,' i, 19—21, ' Knight's Tale,' 1493.
‡ ' Purgatorio,' xii, 19.

In the 'Legend of Good Women,' Chaucer says—

> " Envie is lavendere* of the court alway ;
> For she ne parteth, neither nyght ne day,
> Out of the house of Cesar,—thus seith Dante."

This is a softening of—

> " La meretrice, che mai dall ospizio
> Di Cesare non torse gli occhi putti."†

Longfellow has—

> " The courtesan who never from the dwelling
> Of Cæsar turned her harlot eyes."

Dante has a reference to the Trinity :

> " Quell' uno e due e tre che sempre vive,
> E regna sempre in tre e due e uno,
> Non circonscritto, e tutto circonscrive,
> Tre volte era cantato di ciascuno."‡

This Chaucer utilises at the end of 'Troilus' as an invocation :

> " Thou oon, and two, and three, eterne onlive,
> That regnest ay in three and two and oon,
> Uncirconscript, and al mayst circumscrive,
> Us from visible and invisible foon
> Defende." §

That famous verse of Dante,

> " Nessun maggior dolore,
> Che ricordarsi del tempo felice
> Nella miseria." ‖

---

* Washerwoman. The reference to Dante is wrongly given in the 'Globe' Chaucer, and the quotation is inaccurately printed.

† 'Inferno,' xiii, 64—65.

‡ 'Paradiso,' xiv, 28—30.

§ Foon = Foes.

‖ 'Inferno,' v, 121—123.

may have suggested to Chaucer the words he uses in 'Troilus and Cressida.' *

> " For of fórtunès sharp adversity,
> The worstè kind of ínfortune is this:
> A man to han ben in prosperité,
> And it remembren when it passèd is."

But it may be that he derived the thought, which after all is not very recondite, from Boethius, whom he translated. The opening lines of the ' Purgatorio' probably suggested the opening lines of the second book of " Troilus and Cressida,' but Chaucer's indebtedness here is but for a single phrase. Again in the fourth book (225—227) :

> " And as in winter levès ben biraft,
> Ech after other, til the tree be bare,
> So that ther n'is but bark and braunche y-lafte,"

may have been suggested by Dante's

> " Come d'autunno si levan le foglie
> L'una appresso dell' altra, infin che il ramo
> Vede alla terra tutte le sue spoglie." †

The simile, however, is an obvious one, and at the most the words of Dante can only have reminded Chaucer of what he must himself so often have seen.

In the ' Parlament of Fowls,' which is a poetical abstract of Cicero's ' Somnium Scipionis,' there are traces of Dante's influence. Chaucer places himself under the guidance of Africanus as Dante does

---

* iii, 1625—1628.
† ' Inferno,' iii, 112—114.

under that of Virgil. The inscription over the
entrance to the garden of Venus has, perhaps, been
suggested by the inscription over the entrance to
the Inferno, and there are also five lines which are
certainly translated from Dante. They are not of
first-rate importance.

> " Lo giorno se n'andava e l'aer bruno
>   Toglieva gli animai che sono in terra,
>   Dalle fatiche loro."*

> " The day gan failen, and the derkè nyght,
>   That reveth bestès from hir besynesse."†

> " E poichè la sua mano alla mia pose,
>   Con lieto volto, ond' io mi confortai."‡

> " With that my hond in his he took a-noon,
>   Of which I comfort caughte and went in faste."§

The exact meaning of Lydgate's statement that
Chaucer wrote Dante in English is a matter of con-
troversy. Dr. Skeat sees in it a reference to the
'House of Fame.' Professor Ten Brink regards
that poem as the counterpart, in a light and
humorous vein, of Dante's great work. Dr. Rambeau has collected many passages to show the
indebtedness of Chaucer to the Italian. But the
parallels are not all deadly, and the citations are
not always convincing. Chaucer and Dante both
use as a simile the humming of bees as heard issuing
from the hive. Is it necessary to suppose that the
English poet borrowed from the Italian a simili-
tude that might so often be suggested by the

---

* 'Inferno,' ii, 1—3.   † 'Parlament of Fowles,' 85—86.
‡ 'Inferno,' iii, 19—20.   § Ibid., 169—170.

sights and sounds of his own country? Here are the words :

> "But while that I behold this sight,
> I heard a noise approachen blive
> That fared as been do in a hive,
> Again here time of outflying."*

> "Gia era in loco ove s'udia il ribombo
> Dell' acqua che cadea nell' altro giro,
> Simile a quel che l'arnie fanno rombo."†

The influence of Dante upon Chaucer is indisputable and undisputed, but the extent may easily be exaggerated. The Eagle in the 'House of Fame,' as Prof. Lounsbury points out, owes something to Dante, but, perhaps, still more to Ovid. The same acute critic estimates at twenty the number of lines incontestably due to Dante in this poem, and as to the general resemblances he declares that "in the whole range of imaginative literature there are hardly two poems which exhibit certain superficial resemblances, and one of which has adopted from the other certain passages and images that are most divergent in tone and spirit, in subject and in treatment."‡ Prof. Lounsbury thinks that not more than a hundred lines out of the many thousands written by Chaucer are taken directly from Dante.

Turning from Dante to Petrarca we have to dis-

---

* 'House of Fame,' iii, 430.

† 'Inferno,' xvi, 1—3. The relations of the 'House of Fame' to the 'Divina Commedia' are elaborately discussed in Kolbing's 'Englische Studien,' vol. iii, p. 209, by Dr. A. Rambeau, who estimates Chaucer's indebtedness as much greater than some other critics have allowed.

‡ Lounsbury, ii, p. 247.

cuss the possibility of personal knowledge as well as of literary indebtedness. Chaucer's Monk speaks of " my master Petrarch " * and the Clerk of Oxenford, says :

> " I wol you tell a talè which that I
> Lernèd at Padwè of a worthy clerk,
> As prevèd by his wordès and his werk ;
> He is now deed and naylèd in his cheste,
> I preye to God so yeve his soulè reste !
> Fraunceys Petrak, the lauriat poete,
> Hightè this clerk whose rhetorikè sweet
> Enlumyned al Ytaille of poetrie,—
> As Lynyan dide of philosophie,
> Or lawe, or oother art particuler,—
> But deeth, that wol not suffre us dwellen heer,
> But as it were a twynklyng of an eye,
> Hem bothe hath slayn, and allè shul we dye.
> But forth to tellen of this worthy man
> That taughtè me this tale, as I began,
> I seye that first with heigh stile he enditeth,
> Er he the body of his talè writeth,
> A prohemye, in the which discryveth he
> Pemond, and of Salucès the contree ;
> And speketh of Apennyn, the hillès hye
> That ben the boundes of West Lumbardye,
> And of Mount Vesulus in specïal,
> Where as the Poo out of a wellè smal
> Taketh his firste spryngyng and his sours,
> That estward ay encresseth in his cours
> To Emelward, to Ferrare, and Venyse,—
> The which a longe thyng werè to devyse,
> And trewèly, as to my juggèment,
> Me thynketh it a thyng impertinent,
> Save that he wole convoyen his mateere ;
> But this is his talè which that ye may heere."

* 'Monk's Tale,' 335.

In this passage we have first an interesting frag-
ment of literary criticism, and secondly, what we
should like to think is a piece of autobiography.
The description of the country which Chaucer regarded as not being pertinent to the story of
Griseldis is not in the Italian text of Boccaccio.
The criticism is more applicable to Petrarca's Latin
version which Chaucer used, though the topo-
graphical matter which he has introduced only
amounts to less than a score of lines.

May we identify the poet with the Clerk of
Oxenford and say that Chaucer learned the pathetic
story of Griselda from Petrarca at Padua? The
thought of so picturesque a conjunction carries with
it the desire to believe. There are two occasions on
which it has been suggested they may have met.
The first is at the marriage of the Duke of Clarence
and Violante Visconti in 1368. It has been argued
that Chaucer was not present at this ceremony, as
there are entries among the issue rolls which show
that his pension was drawn in London. Mr.
Hamilton Bromby, however, has satisfied himself
that there is in these documents a significant omission of the words *per manus proprias*, from which
he argues that the money was paid to a representative and not to the poet himself. Presumably,
therefore, as he was not in London he may have
been at Milan. But Signor Carlo Segrè contends
that Petrarca was not present at the marriage, but
was then engaged on a diplomatic errand at Padua.
Petrarca, it is noted, writing a gossiping letter to
his friend Francesco Bruni on other matters has not
a word to say about the Milan festivities, where it

7

has been asserted he was treated with great distinction and placed at the table with princes. The
interview may possibly have taken place at Padua
in 1373,* when Chaucer was in Italy as one of a
commission to arrange for a settlement of Genoese
merchants in England. These envoys left this
country at the end of 1372, and Chaucer was again
at home in November, 1373, when he personally received his half-yearly pension. As Petrarca finished
his Latin version of ' Griselda,' in June, 1373, there
is a possibility, and, indeed, a great probability, that
he would repeat this pathetic story " to a learned
visitor who had come out of his way to see him."
The English poet's reference to Padua is justified
by Segrè, who says that during the time when it
would be possible for Chaucer to see him Petrarca
was not at Arqua, as has sometimes been supposed,
but at Padua. It was not until September or
October, 1373, that Petrarca returned to Arqua
where he died in August, 1374.

The apparent obligations of Chaucer to Petrarca
are not great, and are certainly not so large as to
Boccaccio, of whom he makes no mention. This
silence is remarkable and is so unusual with Chaucer
as to need an explanation which in the present state
of our knowledge it is impossible to give. It has
been suggested that Chaucer may have had a copy
of those writings of Boccaccio of which he certainly
made use, bound up with others of Petrarca and all

* The question is discussed in the ' Athenæum,' No. 3699, Sept.
17, 1898, (C. H. Bromby); No. 3700, Sept. 24 (C. H. Bromby) No.
3706, Nov. 5 (St. Clair Baddeley); No. 3708, Nov. 19 (C. H. Bromby);
No. 3710, Dec. 3 1898 (St. Clair Baddeley); ' Nuova Antologia,'
Gennaio, 1899 (Carlo Segrè).

under the name of Petrarca, and that he therefore
sometimes supposed himself to be quoting Petrarca,
when he was really making use of Boccaccio.   This
is not so improbable as at first might be supposed.
The attribution of the writings of one man to
another would not be difficult in MS. copies, and
Mr. W. M. Rossetti has pointed out that in a French
prose version of the 'Filostrato,' the translator,
Pierre, Seigneur de Beauveau, distinctly affirms that
it was "written by a Florentine poet named
Petrarca."   What Chaucer certainly drew from
Petrarca's Italian writings is a translation of
Sonnet cii.

"S' amor non è, che dunque è quel ch' i' sento ?"

This occurs in 'Troilus and Cressida,' which is
adapted from the 'Filostrato.' The curious point
is that Chaucer says the sonnet is by Lollius, a
ghost-author, of whom nothing can be made.   The
three references to this alleged Lollius are to one
who has written on the history of Troy, to the
original authority for 'Troilus and Cressida,' and
to the author of the love song.   Here the second
reference is to Boccaccio and the third as certainly
to Petrarca.   Then comes Lydgate with the statement that Chaucer in his youth translated from the
Lombard tongue a book called 'Trophe,' to which
at the later period he gave the name of 'Troilus
and Cressida.'   Chaucer, as we have already seen,
elsewhere mentions Trophe as an author to whom
he is indebted for information as to the pillars of
Hercules.   It has been suggested that Chaucer

misunderstood the opening lines of the second epistle of the first book of Horace, which is addressed to Lollius, but this, with what is known of his knowledge of Latin, seems improbable. Prof. Lounsbury says it is doubtful if Chaucer possessed a copy of Horace,* but this particular passage he may have seen in the 'Polycraticus' of John of Salisbury, with which we know he was acquainted.† By the aid of the wandering Greek scholar Leontius Pilatus, Boccaccio made a prose transcript of the 'Iliad' and 'Odyssey' which he sent to Petrarca. It seems certain that by Lollius is meant Petrarca and Boccaccio. But even if we suppose that Chaucer had these writings of Boccaccio in a MS. bearing the name of Petrarca, there is no explanation of the causes which led him to use the name of Lollius for either, or both, of these Italian authors.

Chaucer's indebtedness to Boccaccio is much greater than to Dante or Petrarca. We think now of Boccaccio as the prose novelist, but to Chaucer he was the poet and the scholar. From his 'Teseide' the English bard has taken the plot and something more of the 'Knight's Tale,' but the extent of his borrowing may easily be exaggerated. The Italian poem extends to 9896 lines whilst the English one has only 2250. Of these Mr. Henry Ward has shown that 270 are directly translated, 374 have a general resemblance and 132 a slight likeness. Thus two thirds of the poem are independent of

---

* Lounsbury, ii, pp. 261—264, 410. Skeat, ii, p. 52.

† It is quoted by him, lib. vii, cap. ix. This has been pointed out by the present writer in 'Notes and Queries,' 9th S., iii.

Boccaccio's verse. The story and the general arrangement of the 'Knight's Tale' are undoubtedly due to Boccaccio's 'Teseide.' The English poet, it is believed, first wrote 'Palamon and Arcite' in seven line stanzas, and some fragments have found their way into other poems. Then at a later date the story was rewritten to form the 'Knight's Tale.' *

In addition to the use made of the "Teseide" in the 'Knight's Tale,' passages from it have been used by Chaucer elsewhere. Thus stanzas 51—66 of the 'Teseide' appear with some rearrangement in 27—29, 31—42 of the 'Parlament of Fowls.' The first three stanzas of 'Anelida and Arcite' are taken from the opening of the 'Teseide,' and the eighth, ninth, and tenth stanzas of the English poem are near enough to the eleventh and twelfth stanzas of the second book of the Italian to establish Chaucer's use of them. In the 'Troilus and Cressida,' stanza 1, book v, is taken from stanza 10 of book ix, of 'Teseide,' and stanza 2, book v, from the Italian stanza 1, book ii. Chaucer's stanzas 259, 260, 261, are taken from Boccaccio's stanzas 1—3, book ix. 'Troilus and Cressida' is founded on the 'Filostrato' of Boccaccio, but instead of an abridgment the English is an amplification of the Italian. Mr. W. M. Rossetti has closely examined the relations of the two, and states as the result that 'Filostrato' contains 5704 lines and 'Troilus' 8239. But only 2730 of the original lines have been used by Chaucer, and these he has made English in 2583 lines. Thus two thirds of Chaucer's poem is independent of Boccaccio.

* Skeat, iii, 389.

In the 'Legend of Good Women,' Cleopatra is said to have prepared a pit of serpents and to have gone into it naked that they might sting her to death as she had resolved not to survive Antony. This account, for which no legendary source has been found, seems to be based on a misapprehension of a stanza in Boccaccio's 'Visione Amorosa.'*

Chaucer has laid under contribution Boccaccio's Latin writings in the 'Monkes Tale, de Casibus Virorum Illustrium.'   The monk's examples of tragedy "of hem that stood in high degree" are taken from the 'Casibus Virorum et Feminarium Illustrium,' and the 'De Claris Mulieribus.' Chaucer, however, uses his material freely, makes additions from Boethius, the 'Roman de la Rose,' and the Bible.

There remains the questions of the indebtedness of Chaucer to the 'Decamerone.' Here the one certain fact is the story of 'Griseldis.' Although Boccaccio's novels were written about 1350—1353 they were not known to Petrarca until 1373. The humanist had no great sympathy for these stories which were intended not for the learned, but for the general public, and were written in the vulgar tongue. To us Petrarca is known by his Italian verse, but to his own generation he was the scholar, writing, as was then the scholar's custom, if not duty, in Latin. Moreover, as the shadows were gathering round Petrarca, the lighter vein and the indecorum of many of Boccaccio's tales may have jarred upon his feelings. But one story he found

* See a letter of Mr. F. J. Mather, jun., in the 'New York Nation,' Oct., 1898.

which differed from the rest, and this affected him
so powerfully that he made a translation of it into
what was then the common language of the world
of literature and learning. It is Petrarca's Latin
version of 'Griseldis' that Chaucer has followed.*

Although Chaucer's temperament would make
him more open to its influence, there is no decisive
evidence that he was acquainted with the 'Decamerone' even by name. If Petrarca did not
know this work of one who was his friend and cor-
respondent there is nothing remarkable in the
ignorance of an Englishman who was only a visitor
to Italy and made no lengthy stay. It has been
thought that the framework of the 'Canterbury
Tales' was suggested by that of the 'Decamerone.'
This is possible, but there is no evidence that can
be cited in proof. Boccaccio was not the first, nor
Chaucer the last, to arrange a series of stories
bound together by connecting dialogue and en-
closed in a general narrative. Few, if any, of these
frameworks are so probable and so natural as that
devised by Chaucer. It may indeed be objected
that it would be difficult for all the motley company
to hear the narration, and the length of some of the
tales may strike the modern reader as wearisome
for a wayside diversion. Certainly such story telling is now, for good or evil, a lost art.

Professor Lounsbury does not hesitate to declare
that " there is not a particle of evidence that Chaucer
had ever seen or read a line of the 'Decameron.'"

---

* Petrarca's letter, his Latin version of 'Griseldis,' and the Italian
text of Boccaccio are very conveniently brought together for
Chaucer students in the "Originals and Analogues" already cited.

There, however, are certain of Chaucer's tales which bear a more or less resemblance to stories in 'Boccaccio,' and to these we may now refer.

The story of the trick played upon Puccio by his wife and Don Felice (Gior. iii, Nov. 4) may possibly have given some slight suggestion for the 'Miller's Tale,' but the resemblance is far too shadowy to be strongly insisted upon. The coarse but humorous 'Reeve's Tale' is undoubtedly the same in its main incidents as the story which Boccaccio tells of Pinuccio, Niccolosa, and Adriano (Gior. ix, Nov. 6). As the tale did not originate with the Italian author, but is found in a fabliau of Jean de Boves and in other places, Chaucer need not be supposed to have taken it from the 'Decameron.' In the details the English poet is closer to the fabliau than to the novella. In later times it is found in the 'Cent Nouvelles Nouvelles' and in Lafontaine.* The 'Shipman's Tale' has in its motive a certain resemblance to Boccaccio's story of Gulfardo (Gior. viii, Nov. 1), yet says Prof. Skeat, "it is not at all acknowledged that Chaucer took this from the 'Decameron,' which he seems never to have read." It has been retold by Lafontaine and others.

The 'Merchant's Tale' of January and May contains the well-known incident of the pear-tree which is told by Boccaccio of Nicostrato and Lidia (Gior. vii, Nov. 9). The story as told by Chaucer varies from that of Boccaccio, nor can the Italian be

---

* See Dunlop's 'History of Prose Fiction,' edited by H. Wilson. 1888, vol. ii, p. 135; and Landau's 'Quellen des Dekameron,' 2te Auf., Stuttgart, 1884, p. 151.

regarded as its inventor. On the contrary, it is found in varying forms in mediæval fabliaux, and also in oriental collections. There need be no doubt that the narrative travelled from east to west, and may well have been known to Chaucer from other sources than the ' Decamerone.'* The incident has been utilised also by Lafontaine and other writers of a later age. Of the " enchanted tree," Mr. W. A. Clouston has collected various Eastern analogues.†

The ' Franklin's Tale ' resembles one that has been twice told by Boccaccio, once in the ' Filocopo ' and again in the ' Decamerone ' (Gior. x, Nov. 5), yet here we have a distinct statement by Chaucer that he is following a Breton lay. The Oriental elements in the story have been carefully examined by Mr. W. A. Clouston. The power of creating magic gardens and pleasaunces was attributed to Albertus Magnus and Faustus. Humboldt has made the very rationalistic and unromantic suggestion that these marvels are only exaggerated statements of the effects produced by hot-houses in the cultivation of flowers.‡

One of the most striking and picturesque of the incidents narrated by Chaucer is that which forms the ' Pardoner's Tale.' Three men of dissolute life, drunkards and gamblers, find a treasure as they are journeying together. They draw lots as to which of them shall go to the nearest town for food and

* Dunlop, ii, p. 121, Landau 79. ' Originals and Analogues,' pp. 177—348.

† Ibid., p. 343.

‡ Ibid., ii, p. 139—140. ' Originals and Analogues,' p. 291

wine, whilst the others remain to guard the unexpected gold. Whilst the youngest is away on
his errand his fellow rogues agree to murder him
on his return, in order to have his share of the
booty to divide between them. He on his part
decides to poison them in order to remain sole
master of the treasure. Thus all three perish by
violent death. There is a passage in the prologue
describing the false relics which form part of the
Pardoner's stock-in-trade. This may be paralleled
by a passage in Boccaccio (Gior. vi, Nov. 10)
which excited the disapprobation of the Council of
Trent, but the satire is so obvious that there is no
necessity to suppose that the English poet was here
indebted to the Italian novelist. The plot of the
'Pardoner's Tale' is almost identical with one in
the 'Cento Novelle Antiche.' Chaucer tells us
that the scene of the tragedy was Flanders, whilst
in the 'Cento Novelle Antiche' (Nov. 83) the
incident is associated with the name of Christ.
According to this story, as Jesus was walking with
His disciples in a desert place they saw some golden
coins lying on the ground. The disciples wished
to take the gold for their needs, but Jesus said,
"You would take that which takes from our kingdom the greater number of the souls of men. As
we return you will see." Soon afterwards two
boon companions found the treasure. One went
to fetch a mule to carry it away, whilst the other
remained to guard it. The first one brought a
mule and also two loaves of bread. "I had something to eat in the town, but I have brought this
food for you," he says. The second one refuses to

eat until they have loaded the mule, and takes the opportunity, as his companion is stooping, to stab him. Having killed him, the murderer eat one of the loaves and gave the other to the mule, and both fell dead, as the bread had been poisoned. On their return journey Jesus points out to his disciples the treasure still lying there with the corpses beside it. There are Persian variants, one of them by Attar the poet, in which the legend is also associated with the name of Jesus.* Mr. W. A. Clouston has investigated the history of this curious story. In its earliest known form it is found in the 'Vedabha Jataka,' one of the Buddhist birth stories, and from India possibly passed into Persia. An Arabian variant also contains the name of Jesus. Different Arabic versions are to be found in the Calcutta and Bulak and Breslau editions of the 'Arabian Nights.' There is also a Kashmirian variant. With Buddhism the story reached Tibet. By what route it travelled from East to West is not clear. Italy supplies three forms, and there are also German, French, and Portuguese variants. It cannot be said that any one of the stories cited is certainly, or even probably, the source of Chaucer's 'Pardoner's Tale,' which is most likely

* The sayings attributed to Jesus, but not recorded in the Gospels, and the legendary incidents associated with his name by uncanonical and non-Christian writers, would form an interesting study. The discovery of the 'Logia Iesou' has called renewed attention to the first, to which Resch's 'Agrapha' is the best guide. Dr. Margoliouth in the 'Expository Times' 1894, has treated of "Christ and Islam." Two of El Ghazzali's anecdotes of Jesus are translated in my 'Ancoats Skylark' pp. 53 and 93. The account of Christ in Tabari's great chronicle is curious, and still more so is the Jewish tradition embodied in the "Toldoth Jeschu."

based upon a recension still undiscovered. And it is of course possible that he learned it from conversation, and not from a book.*

We have now before us the material points of the evidence which proves the nature and the extent of the Italian influence upon Chaucer. One of the first things that will strike the inquirer is the freedom and mastery of Chaucer. He is neither a servile imitator nor a mere transcriber of other men's thoughts, but one who moulds the materials into fresh shapes, and stamps it with his own artistic individuality. Opinions have varied greatly as to the degree of Chaucer's indebtedness, and it has therefore been thought best *here* not to insist upon more than the acknowledged minimum. It is best in disputable matters to be guided by the most cautious spirit of criticism. There will be no quarrel with those who are disposed to think that quantitatively Chaucer's obligations should be rated higher. The real effect on the mind of the poet need not be measured by the number of lines that can be traced to their Italian original. " It was," as Prof. Lounsbury has well said, " a spiritual influence even more than a purely intellectual one that was exerted over him by the great Italian writers. By them his views of his art were broadened and enlarged. Through them his power of expression gained fuller and ampler development. To them he owed especially an immeasurable increase in his capacity to

* See 'Originals and Analogues' pp. 29, 415, 544. The Italian forms are in the 'Cento Novelle Antiche' (Nov. 83), the 'Libro di Novelle e di Bel Parler' (lxxxii), and the Italian miracle play of St. Antony.

deal with the deeper problems of man's life and destiny." *

It is a notable circumstance that whilst the French and many of the Latin authors to whom Chaucer was more or less indebted have passed into oblivion, the Italian writers are still the great names of the literature of their fatherland. Jehan de Meung and Marie de France are but names, except to the most diligent explorers of the byways of learning, but the fame of Dante, Boccaccio, and Petrarca, instead of diminishing, has grown greater with the revolving centuries. And this may justify us in thinking that there is a difference in kind between the effect on Chaucer's mind of the men of talent from whom he took more, and the men of genius from whom he took less, but whose influence penetrated deeper into his spirit and more profoundedly affected his artistic methods and his outlook on life. The flaming torch of Dante threw a bright light on heights and depths that the puny lanterns of Machault and his compeers could not illuminate. And from Petrarca and Boccaccio he would gain insight into the tragedy, the pathos, and the humour of human life. From these mighty spirits Chaucer would learn the first lesson that genius needs—the lesson of what genius can do.

With Chaucer we begin the story of modern English literature. With Chaucer also begins that study and appreciation of Italian literature which, from the fourteenth to the end of the nineteenth century, has never become extinct, and now, after a period of partial waning, is again waxing and increas-

* Lounsbury, ii, 224.

ing.   Dante and Chaucer will be household names to the end of time, and, as long as their fame endures, they will form a bond of sympathy, spiritual and intellectual, between the English and Italian races.   May that sympathy never die, but ever grow from more to more.

THE PORTRAITS OF GEOFFREY CHAUCER.

BY M. H. SPIELMANN.

WHEN Chaucer lived—and Hafiz of Persia was the setting sun that heralded the decadence of Eastern poetry—the renascence of the Arts in the West was engaging the attention and inflaming the enthusiasm of Occidental Europe. Petrarch, Boccaccio, and Froissart were all working abroad; Langland was entertaining the English world with his 'Vision of Piers Plowman,' and Sir John Mandeville with his 'Travels in the East;' and John Gower, Wycliffe, and Lydgate made their appeal variously to the mind and conscience of the thinking public. The great schism in the Church took place—there were Popes at Rome and Avignon, and the papal tribute had been discontinued : Urban VI was acknowledged by England, Germany, Italy, Hungary, Portugal, and the North ; while Clement VII was revered by France, Spain, and Naples. The power of the Medici family rose and triumphed in Tuscany before Genoa was humbled by Venice ; and University Colleges were founded in rapid succession—Cracow, Heidelberg, and Prague before Chaucer's birth, and during his lifetime Pavia (Vienna), Winchester, Pesth, Cologne, Erfurt, Ferrara, Angers, and Turin. Gunpowder was invented, the Order of the Garter was instituted, and—the vine was planted in Tokay. Intellectual movement was wide-spread, consequent on strife of opinion or as the result of scientific, philosophic, or artistic research, and, above all, the world was rapidly becoming pregnant with the crowning art of printing.

The plastic and the graphic arts, and the arts of design, were included in the general activity. Yet Giotto, the father of modern portrait-painting from the life, and the friend of Dante and Petrarch, had died in 1336, and had left no obvious successor, for Masaccio was not born till two years after Chaucer's death. The Academy of Saint Luke had been founded in Florence in 1350; and Melchior Broederlam of Ipres, the official painter of Philip, Duke of Burgundy, was preparing the way for the improvements in painting that were introduced by the brothers Van Eyck. In England, however, accurate portrait rendering was not widely appreciated; the true *statuæ iconicæ*—or, as Suetonius called them, *simulacra iconica*—were rarely asked for, and, it may be conceived, were still more rarely produced.

Of portraiture of the time of Chaucer we have in England a fairly numerous collection, beginning with the large distemper representation of Richard II in the Sacrarium at Westminster; but even though the supposititious sitters are known—or probably merely guessed at—it is impossible to assert that their portraits were drawn from the life, even from statues, tombs, brasses, or church windows.   In extremely few cases can the name of the painter be ventured upon, with such rare exceptions as " Luca Cornellis's " portrait of John of Gaunt, Duke of Lancaster, now (or lately) in the possession of the Duke of Beaufort.   In such circumstances, it is obvious that without laboured proof of the contrary even the earliest portraits of Chaucer would be open to the suspicion of not being painted from the life, inasmuch as the handling, skilful as it is up to a certain point, is usually roughly executed, in crude masses or touches of colour, or with coarse markings in place of the careful modelling and intelligent effort at characterisation which are commonly to be found in the least capable portraits taken from the living model. There is, perhaps, just the bare possibility that, apart from the Occleve illumination, one of the portraits I am about to mention—the Seddon, or Fairfax Murray portrait—may have been executed by a limner who had seen Chaucer in the flesh.   Although nearly every student of Chaucer and of the history of art would reject the supposition, this view has been supported by at least one distinguished painter ; but it is, of course, impossible to do more than speculate upon the point.   The Occleve portrait, it must be remembered, is admittedly a memory painting, being, however, the only one which is universally accepted as trustworthy.

Although our knowledge of Chaucer and his life is derived mainly from sources other than the direct references vouchsafed to us by his contemporaries and immediate successors (more profuse, nevertheless, than such as we have of Spenser's life), those pieces of information which are not manifestly erroneous are of extreme value. Occleve has a double claim on our gratitude in virtue of portraits both in pen and pencil, descriptive and pictorial. His admiration of Chaucer, whom he calls " maister dere and fader reverent," was unbounded; for, like Leonardo da Vinci, the Father of English Poetry was a man of infinite parts, not a poet only, but a soldier and a scientist, as well as valet and esquire of the King's household, frequently entrusted with missions as envoy and ambassador, employed as Clerk of the Works,* and as Comptroller of the Customs, as well as Member of Parliament; and these abilities, reinforcing his exquisite sense of poetry, commanded the hero-worship of his follower.

It will be remembered that Chaucer, in the ' Canterbury Tales,' is said to have described himself as corpulent, with a small face and elvish, with a habit of looking on the ground—" olde and unlusty " at fifty-two. Hallam, in ' The Middle Ages,' expresses the opinion that Chaucer, to whom he allows vivacity of imagination and ease of expression, lacked " grandeur," as if, like Napoleon Bonaparte when he waxed fat, he lost that highest development of intellectual power and alertness which are popularly supposed to be characteristic

* ' Punch ' (1843) quaintly refers to this occupation: Chaucer " was made Clerk of the Works at Westminster, a situation now held by one of the men in the employ of Messrs. Grissel and Peto."

On page 115, line 10 from bottom, *for* 'De Regimine Principis,' *read* 'De Regimine Principum.'

rather of the ascetic than the obese. But is the description of the poet really a portrait of himself at all? And what reason is there to suppose that the Master of the Ceremonies has the author in view when he banters the rhymester thus?—

> "Now ware you, sirs, and let this man have space,
> He in the waist is shapen as well as I;
> This were a puppet in an arm to embrace
> For any woman, small, and fair of face.
> He seemeth elvish by his countenance,
> For unto no wight doth he dalliance."

By "elvish," Tyrwhitt declares, Chaucer meant "shy and reserved." Yet if we look elsewhere (in the "Prologe of the Chanounes Yeman") the word is used in the commoner sense of "supernatural" or "fairy-like." It may be asked whether the commentator has not been less rigid in respect of Chaucer's language than observant in the matter of his portraits.

I.—The best likeness that is presented to us of Chaucer, then, is the limning, or what we would nowadays call "water-colour drawing," which he introduced into his book 'De Regimine Principis.' In that part of it entitled "De Consilio habendo in omnibus factis" he has executed, or caused to be executed, a fine marginal painting in colours. This is here reproduced from a photograph taken with the latest improvements, so that the relative tones and values may be set forth on the page in a degree of perfection and completeness never before attained. This painting, it will be seen, appears opposite to the following lines:

" Although his lyfe be queynt the resemblaunce
    Of him hath in me so fressh lyflynesse
    That to putte othir men in remembraunce
    Of his p[er]sone I haue heere his lyknesse
    Do make to this ende in sothfastnesse
    That thei that haue of him lest thought & mynde
    By this peynture may ageyn him fynde ".

Occleve then proceeds to justify the painting of
portraits—the art to which Chaucer himself so frequently refers—and to refute the opinion held by
some " that none ymages shuld ymaked be," concluding :

" Passe over that now blessid trinite
    Uppon my maistres soule m[er]cy haue
    ffor him lady eke thi m[er]cy I craue".

It is hardly likely that a portrait undertaken and
executed in this reverent and loving spirit could be
otherwise than a likeness, not only as good as the
artist could paint, but good enough, moreover, to
satisfy him that—

" Whan a thing depeynt is
    Or entailed if men take of it heede
    Thoght of the lyknesse it wil in him brede".

Concerning this portrait Sir Harris Nicolas
says : *
    " The affection of Occleve has made Chaucer's
person better known than that of any individual of
his age.   The portrait . . . is taken from Occleve's
painting already mentioned in the Harleian MS.

See the Aldine Edition of Chaucer's Works (G. Bell and Sons).

PLATE I.

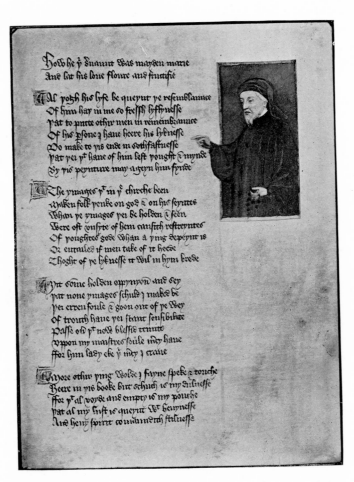

 Adlard & Son, Imp.

4866, which he says was painted from memory after Chaucer's decease, and which is apparently the only genuine portrait in existence. The figure, which is half-length, has a background of green tapestry. He is represented with grey hair and beard, which is bi-forked [like that of his own Marchaunt], he wears a dark-coloured dress and hood, his right hand is extended, and in his left he holds a string of beads. From his vest a black case is suspended, which appears to contain a knife, or possibly 'a penner,'* or pencase. The expression of the countenance is intelligent; but the fire of the eye seems quenched, and evident marks of advanced age appear on the countenance. This is incomparably the best portrait of Chaucer yet discovered."

As to this description, Nicolas is justifiably contradicted by Professor A. Ward,† and by Mr. Thomas R. Lounsbury in his elaborate work upon the poet.‡ Since Nicolas wrote, the discussion as to Chaucer's age has arisen, and perhaps a different view of the portrait has followed the readjustment of dates. Professor Ward concedes the greyness of hair and beard, but very properly " denies that this fact could be taken of itself to contradict the supposition that he died about the age of sixty."

It will, of course, be observed that the extended right hand is pointing out of the picture towards

---

* Compare—
> " Prively a penner gan he borwe
> And in a lettre wrote he all his sorwe."
> > ' Marchaunt's Tale,' l. 9753.

† " English Men of Letters " Series.
‡ ' Studies in Chaucer ' (Harper and Brothers).

the text which describes the portrait, an arrangement more ingenious than artistic.

Dr. Furnivall, the head of the Chaucer Society, emphatically declares that " Occleve's portrait of Chaucer is surely one of a man not above sixty. He doubtless painted his master as he saw him, shortly before his death." * With this view most persons now agree. I may add that Dr. Furnivall tells me he regards as trustworthy no other existing portrait.

As to this limning, one critic has declared that Chaucer's " disciple Occleve *caused* a picture of him to be painted at the beginning of a manuscript of his book ' De Regimine Principis,' which he presented to Henry V." As the writer proceeds to say that " *under* the drawing he inscribed the following stanza," we might hesitate to accept without question the argument of so inaccurate an observer. Yet it cannot be denied, as I have already hinted, that the expression "I have here his likeness do make " may be intended as a disclaimer of original authorship. George Vertue maintains the tradition of genuineness on his principal print of Chaucer, which was No. 2 (John Gower being No. 1, and Edmund Spenser No. 3) in the set executed within ornamental borders with Lord Oxford's arms. Vertue, it may here be stated, engraved another " Geofry Chaucer," large, in an oval frame, as well as a third, smaller, with the verses in old character. Referring to the Occleve drawing, Walpole reminds us that " Urry and Tanner both mention such a

* " Date of Chaucer's Birth," by Dr. F. J. Furnivall, ' Notes and Queries,' 4th s., vii, May 13th, 1871, p. 412.—M. H. S.

portrait, which places Occleve in the rank of one of
our first painters as well as poets." *

Copies of the Occleve portrait are to be found in
one or two of the poet's MSS., and one of them is
engraved to illustrate Tyrwhitt's edition of 'The
Canterbury Tales.' It should here be mentioned
that J. Thomson engraved, " from a limning in
Occleve's Poems in the British Museum," a portrait
on steel " under the superintendence of the Society
for the Diffusion of Useful Knowledge," and it was
issued in the third volume of 'The Gallery of
Portraits, with Memoirs,' published by C. Knight,
22, Ludgate Hill, 1834, and republished in 1853 by
W. S. Orr. The engraving shows a man of about
seventy years, with a nose inclined to be aquiline,
and with white hair. The face is in stipple.

Houbraken and George Vertue both engraved a
plate after the Occleve portrait. Each man worked
for Knapton ; the former was the finer artist, the latter the more conscientious. " Some of Houbraken's
heads," says Walpole, " were carelessly done, especially of the moderns ; but Vertue had a fault to
dealers which was a merit to the public : his scrupulous veracity could not digest imaginary portraits,
as some of those engraved by Houbraken. . . .
Vertue was *incommode;* he loved truth." The
undertaking referred to was entitled 'Heads of
Illustrious Persons of Great Britain,' with lines by
Dr. Birch, and it was completed in 1752.

Houbraken's plate shows a man about fifty years
of age, with whiskers, moustache, and beard,
looking to the right, being, doubtless, not first

* Walpole's 'Anecdotes of Painting,' vol. i, p. 31.

reversed by the careless artist when engraving on the copper direct from the painting. The face is somewhat wrinkled, and the nose is straight with a well-defined bridge and an end inclined to be bulbous. S. Freeman engraved the same portrait, and his plate was published by Archibald Fullarton and Co., of Glasgow, in Cunningham's 'Lives of Eminent Englishmen,' 1836. A third plate, in which a column, a curtain, and a church, with a landscape background, were added—in the manner of the Clarendon Portrait—was issued by Darton, of Holborn Hill; but the likeness had degenerated into a caricature. Other subsequent versions exist to which it is needless to refer.

George Vertue's plate, with Occleve's lines beneath, was published in 'Ancient British Portraits,' issued or reissued by Boydell in 1812. It also shows, curiously enough, a small whisker; the figure is a quarter-length, without hands, and is inserted in a bad architectural border, and inscribed "Ad exemplar Thomæ Occleve in libro suo, DE REGIMINE PRINCIPIS, Walliæ Principis (postea Hen. V) inscripto." "Ectypum hoc alim dum in vivis destinatum nunc τᾶ μακαριζ a memoriæ consecratum esse volui. G. Vertue." It need only be added that the Roxburghe Club issued the Occleve poem in 1860; and that the whisker, so far as the Occleve portraits are concerned, is entirely without authority.

II.—In a copy of Occleve's poems, in the Royal MS. 17, D vi. F 90ᴮ, in the British Museum (Department of Manuscripts), is a full-length portrait, which in Nicolas's opinion is very early, if no

PLATE II.

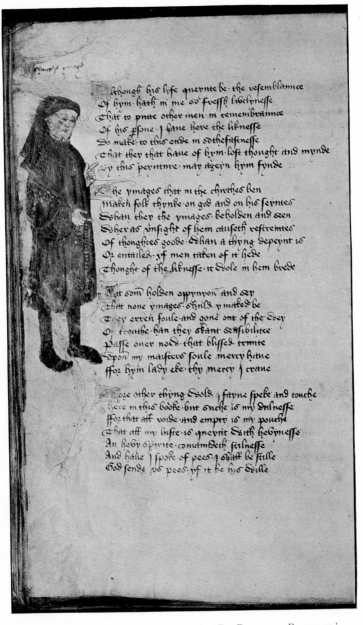

FROM THE MINIATURE IN OCCLEVE'S 'DE REGIMINE PRINCIPIS.'
ROYAL MS. 17 D, VI, F 90^{B}. BRITISH MUSEUM.

actually contemporaneous with Occleve himself. I doubt, however, if Nicolas ever examined this portrait with his own eyes. In his description he says : " He appears very old, with grey hair and beard : he holds a string of beads in his left hand, and his right arm is extended as if speaking earnestly. His vest, hood, stockings, and pointed boots are all black. Over the figure is written, in the same hand as the poems, ' Chaucers ymage.' "

Now the reader can satisfy himself from the reproduction here that the string of beads is held in the *right* hand, and that the left arm is *not* " extended " (as is the case in MS. 4866—the original Occleve) ; and, indeed, that the whole figure faces to the right. Moreover, the poet is not supposed to be "speaking earnestly," but is simply pointing to the words " By this peynture." But what will further be noticed is this : that Nicolas makes no reference to the variations in the text, which appears to me of a date much later than that to which he is inclined to attribute it ; that the execution is in all respects less competent and serious than in the original—features and details being alike ill-drawn by comparison ; while the number of twenty-three or twenty-four beads (more resembling counters) in the rosary is probably nearer truth than the ten large balls in the portrait first described. Above all, I would direct attention to the strange drawing of the feet. The left foot is not more uncouth in shape than the character of the boot and the draughtsmanship of the period would explain ; but the toes of the right foot turn up curiously. This might not be regarded as a

noteworthy circumstance were it not for the fact—
not hitherto recognised, so far as I am aware—that
other full-length portraits invite attention to a
similar peculiarity. I come back to this point later
when discussing the picture at the National Portrait Gallery, comparing it with others similarly
suggestive; but I would hazard the theory that it
was this short-leggedness which inspired the artist
of the Ellesmere MS. to show on horseback a bigly
made man with the leg of a dwarf.

III.—A portrait pleasing in arrangement, but
lacking in character, is the small full-length which
is best known to the reading public through the
coloured illustration (rather too brightly illuminated
in lithography) which is reproduced in ' Dresses and
Decorations of the Middle Ages,' by Henry Shaw,
F.S.A.* This portrait, which is on vellum,
together " with an account of Chaucer in a modern
hand," says Sir Harris Nicolas, " is in the Additional MS. 5141 in the British Museum, and has
lately been engraved [by Shaw]. It is a full-length,
and in one corner is the date 1402, and in another
corner a daisy; but it has no pretensions to the
genuineness of Occleve's painting in the Harleian
MS. 4866, and is perhaps not older than the reign
of Queen Elizabeth."

The portrait, ill enough drawn, and, I take it,
quite as recent as Elizabeth's reign, shows a man in
a brown-grey hood and frock, black hose, and shoes
edged with red. A red tassel hangs from the rosary,
and a red top decorates the inkhorn or penner.
The beard is bi-forked, and the poet has the appear-

* Two vols., Pickering, 1843.—M. H. S.

PLATE III.

1402

FROM THE PORTRAIT IN ADD. MS. 5141. BRITISH MUSEUM.

Adlard & Son, Imp.

PLATE IV.

FROM THE ILLUMINATION IN THE LANSDOWNE MS. 851. BRITISH MUSEUM.

ance of being about forty years of age. The purple daisy, Chaucer's favourite flower, seems to be the *Bellis perennis ;* and the figures in which the date is written probably belong to late in the sixteenth century. It will be observed, by reference to the date and the daisy, that Nicolas is once more loose in his description of the relative position of the accessories.

George Vertue engraved a three-quarter length from the standing figure, but the likeness is a very poor one. The plate was used as a frontispiece to ' The Canterbury Tales.' It may be recorded that an excellent water-colour copy of this drawing, made by Mr. Smith, at one time Keeper of the Prints at the British Museum, is now (1900) in the large collection of Johnsoniana belonging to Mr. A. H. Hallam Murray.

IV.—In an initial letter in the Lansdowne MS. 851, on Folio 2, is a third portrait, small full-length, in a copy of ' The Canterbury Tales,' which was made in the reign of Henry V—or less than fifty years after Chaucer's death. " He is dressed in a long grey gown," says Nicolas, " with red stockings, and black shoes fastened with black sandals round the ankles. His head is bare, and the hair closely cut. In his right hand he holds an open book, and a knife or pencase, as in the other portraits, is attached to his vest."

Again it will be seen that the description by Nicolas, who is usually respected as a close observer, is incorrect. The book is held in both hands, chiefly the left. Although the MS. is undoubtedly an early one, the portrait, as such, is hardly worth serious consideration; indeed, Dr. Furnivall's contemptuous allusion to it as a " stupid peasant thing" is not unmerited.

The same authority refers to a portrait now perished, which once existed in the Colton MS. Otho A. XVIII, but which was burned at the time of the destruction of that library by fire; as well as to the full-length portrait in the Harleian MS. 4826, which was cut out at or before the time of Queen Elizabeth, by some unhappy vandal— " summe furious foole"—against whom a sixteenth century rhymester launched a denunciation in doggrel verse which is read with approval to this day.

V.—The standing portrait, now in the National Portrait Gallery, has obviously common origin with the " Additional 5141," already described ; but it has important variations. Painted on stout oak panel $11\frac{3}{4}$ inches high (sight measurement $10\frac{1}{2}$ inches high), the little full-length has much the same colour scheme—a greyish hood and garment, white edged at the neck, with black hose, and curiously designed black shoes edged with red round the top and about the instep. The hair is lightish brown. The penner is mounted with gold, and is slung from the fourth button with gold thread. It is to be noted that the beads seem to have been painted by a more skilful hand than that which wrought the rest ; indeed, the brilliance of execution with which the objects are rendered is quite remarkable. A Maltese cross of gold is substituted for the tassel, and the glass beads themselves, contrary to other pictures, are in pairs, alternately red and black. It

PLATE V.

FROM THE SLOANE PORTRAIT (320). NATIONAL PORTRAIT GALLERY.

Adlard & Son, Imp.

is very curious that this portrait (which measures $9\frac{7}{8}$ inches from toe to crown), even more than " Add. 5141 " or " 17 D. vi.," shows a forced attitude of the left foot so marked as to make us doubt whether the distortion is merely an eccentricity of the draughtsman's incompetence, or whether the poet did not really walk upon the toes only of that foot through a stiffened ankle or congenital deformity or shortness of leg. This portrait, numbered 320 of the Sir Hans Sloane collection, whence it came, was transferred from the British Museum in 1879. The face appears to be of a man younger by twenty years than that seen in the Occleve portrait ; it is, moreover, much weaker in character than the latter or the Fairfax Murray picture. There is no note of its previous history.

VI.—The Bodleian portrait has made far more claim upon public attention than it can rightly command. It seems to have little enough interest for Sir Harris Nicolas, who passes it over with the statement that an engraving of it forms the frontispiece of Urry's edition of the poet's works, printed in 1721—that edition, by the way, which Tyrwhitt so vigorously assailed. " This, and others in the British Museum and at Knowle," says Sir Harris, " seem to have been all formed from Occleve's painting, long after his time."

This portrait was shown at " The First Special Exhibition of National Portraits " at the South Kensington Museum in 1866, and was thus described : " Three-quarter miniature, looking to r.,[*]

_____
[*] That is to say, the spectator's left.—M. H. S.

white head-covering and dress; inscribed ' Caucer,
1400 ' * Panel, 1 foot 2 inches × 10½ inches." It
should have been added that beneath the white
head-cloak or hood is a dark shadow, or (judged by
the touches) hair, or a cap; that the face has a
darkish beard, pointed rather than bifurcated, a
shovel nose, somewhat protuding eyes, and a flat
cheek—the whole presenting the appearance of a
man of some forty years.   The eyes are dark,
whereas those in the Occleve and the Fairfax Murray
(or Seddon) portraits are distinctly light.   The
shield is in the top left-hand corner—properly
described thus : Per pale argent and gules a bend
counterchanged.   The figuring beneath it is evidently late, intended apparently to record the date
of the poet's death rather than that of the painting
of the picture.   The shield has obviously been
retouched, and, it may be added, the present condition of the picture is very poor—the paint breaking away from the ground in many places.   It is
to be borne in mind that, in spite of the prestige
supposed to belong to it—due chiefly to the dignity
of its present home—no authority is to be attributed
to this large " miniature."

VII.—It was, as far as I have been able to ascertain, so recently as in 1866 that the Fairfax Murray
or Seddon portrait—as it must for convenience be
named—was first exhibited to the public.   It was
lent by Mr. John P. Seddon, the well-known archi-

* This inscription is almost invisible in the excellent photograph
which I have had taken of this portrait.   It occurs on a level a
little lower than the eye, and is in modern characters.   There are
indications of an inscription having formerly existed immediately
below the shield.—M. H. S.

PLATE VI.

FROM THE PORTRAIT MINIATURE IN THE BODLEIAN LIBRARY, OXFORD.

Adlard & Son, Imp.

tect, and, like the last-named, was included in the
first of the three annual loan exhibitions of national
portraits at the South Kensington Museum.   It was
thus described in the catalogue :

" To waist, small life-size, face three quarters to
r. ;* dated 1400.   Panel, 19 by 14.

" Stated to have been preserved for more than
three centuries in the family of Stokes, of Llanshaw Court, Gloucester; given in 1803 to Benjamin
Dyke."

This portrait, to which I have already alluded,
was originally photographed by Mr. Hollyer, but,
by the courteous permission of Mr. Fairfax Murray,
the present owner, who has given me all help and
information in his power, I have had it photographed
again by Mr. Dixon, with the result of bringing out
more details.

In its general arrangement this portrait closely
resembles the Bodleian miniature ; but it is considerably bigger, and the two halves of the bend
sinister upon the shield, although clearly divided as
in the other picture, do not contrast the colours so
plainly.   Although the panel is a larger one, it is
smaller in relation to the figure, and, in fact, the
face is far better drawn, much more lifelike, and
bears a closer resemblance to the Occleve portrait,
on which one might suppose the arrangement of it
to be founded, except as to the cap, the nose, and
the pose of the right hand.   Moreover the angle at
which the face is seen is not the same.   Here the
hood, as well as the dress, is black ; and white or
very fair the beard—reminding us of Green's de-

* The spectator's *left.*—M. H. S.

scription of Chaucer's "silver haires both bright and sheen . . . his beard was white." Mr. Seddon, the former owner, has given me the following information as to its history.

His brother, the late Thomas Seddon—the artist whose "Jerusalem and the Valley of Jehoshaphat" has lately been transferred from the National Gallery to the Tate Gallery at Millbank—died in 1856, leaving in the care of Messrs. Colnaghi a portrait of Chaucer in oil,* on an oak panel, for sale for the benefit of a nephew and niece of his wife, named Bulford, to whom it belonged. Mr. Seddon, on their behalf, offered the picture for sale to the National Portrait Gallery, but the Trustees proposed for it so small a sum, for the curious reason that "it did not look new enough," that Sir George Scharf, the Director, declined to name it. It was put into a new frame, the old one having disappeared, and after the death of the owners was sold to Mr. Fairfax Murray. It measures $19\frac{1}{8}$ inches high by $15\frac{3}{16}$ inches wide (sight measurement, $18\frac{1}{2}$ inches by $14\frac{1}{2}$ inches), and bears on the back an inscription, always faint, and now almost hopelessly illegible, to this effect:

"This picture was presented by Miss Frances Lambert† to Benjamin Dyke on the 6th September, 1803, to perpetuate the memory of her late invaluable relation, Thomas Stokes, Esq., of Llanshaws Court, in the county of Gloucester, where it was

---

* If it is really in oil, as it certainly appears to be, thinly applied, the date is presumably a later addition. Pictures at that date were more commonly painted in tempera.—M. H. S.

† Or "Lumbert."

PLATE VII.

FROM THE SEDDON OR FAIRFAX MURRAY PORTRAIT (MR. FAIRFAX MURRAY).

          Adlard & Son, Imp.

preserved for more than three centuries, as appears
from the inventory of pictures in the possession of
that ancient and respectable family. The date
under the arms was the period when the venerable
Chaucer died, aged seventy-two.* The wood is of
oak, and has nearly or will wear out the paint [sic].
The frame has been repaired with much difficulty.
The picture is to the possessor invaluable, owing to
the purity of friendship which existed between the
living and the dead. Reader, may thy friendship
with whosoever it may be formed be as sincere, and
may no rude or careless hand destroy this ancient
relick. Time perhaps may perish it when thou and
I are lost."

" Mr. Holman Hunt," says Mr. Seddon, " told
me, when he had carefully examined the picture,
that it puzzled him much, because, not being by a
highly skilled painter, it had so many delicate
touches about the eyes and nostrils, etc., that such
a painter could hardly have produced it except from
life." When compared with the smaller picture
from the Bodleian (exhibited on the same occasion)
Mr. Seddon's picture was generally considered to be
the superior work. As to the Bulfords, it may be
mentioned that Mr. Seddon's sister-in-law was a
Mrs. Edmund Bulford, but here all further trace is
lost. It has ignorantly been suggested that this
picture may be the original of that now, or
formerly, in the British Museum, whither, in 1879,
the picture in the National Portrait Gallery was

---

* This was written, of course, before more recent research caused
a readjustment of dates and, consequently, of the poet's years.—
M. H. S.

transferred; but it is quite clear that the critic never compared the two works. Apart from the colour of the hair, the sitter appears to be a man of about forty years of age.

The similarity in attitude and arrangement, and in a far less degree in feature, between this picture and that in the Bodleian is unmistakable. But, as I have remarked, the portrait is infinitely more convincing as a work from life. It should be said that the resemblance to the Sloane portrait is still more striking.

Now it should be observed that, judging from Sir Harris Nicolas's reference to "an original portrait" mentioned by both Urry and Grainger, we may possibly be upon the track of the Fairfax Murray (or Seddon) portrait. It "was said to be in the possession of George Greenwood, of Chasleton, in Gloucestershire." Chasleton is not far from Llanshaw Court. It is true that the writer adds that it was "taken when he was about thirty years old;" nevertheless there would be some presumptive evidence here, but for the colour of the hair. In any case the Fairfax Murray portrait bears a closer resemblance to the Occleve Chaucer than the Bodleian can claim to do; and, ill drawn though it is in the region of the shoulder, the first named is probably the original of the latter. On the other hand, it is not possible to claim for it any positive authority, in spite of its evident antiquity and its claim to a measure of respect.

VIII. Among the most characteristic portraits of Chaucer is the equestrian miniature, represent-

ing the poet as he is supposed to speak of himself
as on horseback journeying with the pilgrims to
Canterbury. This "is preserved in a MS. of his
poems belonging to the Marquis of Stafford, which
has been engraved in 'Todd's Illustrations of
Gower and Chaucer,' 8vo, 1810." * This portrait,
when it came into the possession of Lord Francis
of Egerton, was declared by another critic to be
good as to the face, but the body as remarkably
ill proportioned. "The resemblance which these
different portraits bear to each other leaves no room
to doubt that the likeness is correct." The horse
is white, and the harness black. "His figure," says
Sir Harris Nicolas, "is small, short, and rather
stout: he wears a long dark-coloured dress and
hood, with a girdle, and a purse or gipciere, and
he is booted and spurred." This, known as the
Ellesmere portrait, from its being in the MS. belonging to the Earl of Ellesmere, is the only extra
portrait (so called) which Dr. Furnivall issued for
the Chaucer Society. As the doctor characteristic-
ally writes to me, "It has as much authority as the
Bodleian or Fairfax Murray portraits—that is, none
at all; but is not so ridiculous as the stupid peasant
thing in another British Museum MS.† . . . .
But I think the Ellesmere one represents a man
of Chaucer's type and class on horseback, and is
worth reproducing. Mr. W. Hooper, 5, Hammer-
smith Terrace, has the copy he made from the
MS."

Mr. W. H. Hooper, the well-known engraver,

* See Rev. James Dallaway's Notes.—M. H. S.
† That is to say, the Lansdowne MS. 851. Cf. *supra*.—M. H. S.

tells me : " It is many years since I did the work, which was wrought under difficulties—a bad light for one ; but I did my best to make it accurate as far as its condition permitted. My instructions were to make the drawing good in such places as time and handling had damaged the work. All the figures are drawn on the margin, so they have suffered the more ; the red used was a lead preparation, which had changed to a metallic black, and other colours had turned because of the white used for body being also a lead colour. Dr. Furnivall had photographs taken some years afterwards, which were to be printed in colour ; but a fire occurred which destroyed the printer's shop, so nothing came of it."

I may add that the negative here referred to is now lost—last heard of it was in the possession of Mr. Prætorious—but not before a collotype illustration was made from it. By the courtesy of the Earl of Ellesmere and his trustees I am enabled here to set before the reader an excellent reproduction of this interesting and important limning. This representation is obviously far more truthful than the wood engraving which—on a somewhat enlarged scale, I fancy—Mr. Hooper made of it for the Chaucer Society; not because that skilful engraver was unable to approach in his block more closely to the original, but because it was cut for hand colouring, and not for printing in black and white, a form in which, nevertheless, it was presented to the world. Mr. Hooper cut on wood the whole of the drawings of twenty-three letters to the twenty-four ' Canterbury Tales ' in 1871. The

PLATE VIII.

FROM THE MINIATURE IN ELLESMERE MS. LEAF 157, BACK.
THE EARL OF ELLESMERE, BRIDGEWATER HOUSE.

     Adlard & Son, Imp.

painting in the Ellesmere MS. is on leaf 157, back, and occurs on the left-hand of the page opposite the following lines :

PORTRAIT OF CHAUCER HERE.	A heere bigynneth Chaucers tale of Melibee yong man called Melibeus myghty and riche

It will thus be seen that there is no lack of so-called portraits of Chaucer; copies, and copies of copies, sufficiently alike to confuse the student, yet without difference enough to invest them with the highest historical interest. The majority are at bottom so many acts of reverence to the poet, called forth by the simple desire to have his features reproduced from sheer love of him. Such was "the painted effigies of Chaucer," in full length, of which Walpole speaks—that which "remained within these few years * on his tomb at Westminster,"—a portrait, says Dallaway, which " was copied from some unknown miniature of him, when Nicolas Brigham erected a monument to his memory in Westminster Abbey in 1550,† as the inscription proves, at which time it was painted against the wall. No trace is now visible." And such, too, was Chaucer's statue which the Royal Commission determined (in 1845) to erect in the House of Parliament at Westminster, to the surprise of all practical-minded people. One of these, Percival Leigh, put the general feeling into rhyme in ' Punch,' when he proposed the following inscription should be carved on the statue's

* Circa 1750.
† The correct date is 1556.—M. H. S.

base in what he considered good Chaucerian verse
pour rire :

> "Good Sirs, I marvel what we herè maken,
> Gretè folk, certès, be sometimes mistaken,
> We standen in this stound by much erroùr,
> Ne poet was in Parlement before ;
> We are fysh out of water, verily,
> I do not brethè well this air, perdỳ.
> In the Abbaye we weren well enoughe ;
> To put us here in Parlement is stuffe."

James Elmes, M.R.I.A.,* after foolishly describing the Occleve portrait as " a mere pen-and-ink sketch," proceeds : " About 1802 an early painting of Chaucer, believed to be coeval with his time, was found by Sir Richard Phillips in a lumber garret of the house at Huntingdon in which Oliver Cromwell was born. It is on panel, about three feet six inches by two feet six inches, in the flat and unrelieved style of the early painters, but accompanied by all those minutiæ of still life which characterise their works. The physiognomy is similar to that by Occleve, and the complexion, the hair, and the costume accord with Occleve's description of the poet. Coin lies scattered upon the table, indicative of his employment in the Customs, and he carries the white wand of office in his hand. On a chest is spiritedly sketched his ' Knight's Tale,' and in the background, in legible characters, stands the word 𝕮𝖍𝖆𝖚𝖈𝖊𝖗. If painted in the reign of Richard II, of

---

* 'The Arts and Artists,' vol. iii, p. 70. London : Knight and Lacey, 1825.

which there appears little doubt, it is perhaps the oldest picture in England, and almost the oldest portrait in Europe. Its discovery and acquisition led Sir Richard Phillips to make it the basis of a gallery of original portraits of English poets and men of letters." I have been unable to trace this remarkable work; and I may add that I am hardly convinced of its existence, or, at least, of its genuineness.

IX. Apocryphal and mythical portraits are hardly less perplexing than those which apparently are lost. Among these has been reckoned the supposed medal or medallion to which John Evelyn is thought by some to refer in his letter of the 12th August, 1689, written from Sayes Court to Mr. Samuel Pepys. Discussing the collecting of portraits in a long argument full of intelligence and understanding, he says : " At present I know of none who can show a better chosen set of Medals than the Earle of Clarendon "—that is to say, the second Earl (Lord Cornbury), whose father, the Lord Chancellor, conceived the " purpose to furnish all roomes of state and other apartments with the Pictures of our most Illustrious of our Nation, especially of his Lordship's time and acquaintance, and of diuers before it." After enumerating a long list of portraits, he adds : " And what was most agreable to his Lordship's general humour, Old Chaucer, Shakspere, Beaumont and Fletcher, who were both in one piece."

If the work here mentioned could have reference to a medal at all—the word " picture " being an elastic term with some—such a work is not to be found. The present Earl of Clarendon (to whom, for the mere sake of accuracy and completeness, I applied) knows nothing of it; nor, moreover, is there any trace of it or of any other Chaucer medal in the British Museum. It may, in fact, be mentioned that Chaucer lived at a time far anterior to that at which the art of the medallist was introduced into England, for the earliest contemporary portrait-medal of an Englishman is that of John Kendal, executed in 1450. Evelyn adds that most of the portraits he mentions, "if not all, are at the present at Cornebery in Oxfordshire." Now, when Cornbury's owner sold the estate to George Duke of Marlborough, the great-grandfather of the present Lord Spencer-Churchill, the pictures were removed, as is stated later.

As a matter of fact, John Evelyn did not refer to a medal at all, but to the picture which Lady Theresa Lewis, in her 'Lives of the Friends and Contemporaries of Lord Chancellor Clarendon,' declares to have been removed to Bothwell Castle. This picture still hangs upon the walls of the castle, and by the kindness of the owner, the Earl of Home, and with the consent of the lessee, Sir James King, Bt., I have been enabled to have it photographed and here placed before the reader— the first time, I believe, that the work has ever been reproduced. Lord Home reminds me that "the picture came into the possession of the family with the rest of the collection at Bothwell Castle, which consists of half the Chancellor Clarendon's collection left to the family by the Duke of Queensberry and Dover." That is to say that one half of that

PLATE IX.

THE CLARENDON PORTRAIT. THE EARL OF HOME, BOTHWELL CASTLE.

Adlard & Son, Imp.

collection is at Bothwell Castle, and the other at
The Grove, Watford.

The picture is on canvas, four feet two inches by
three feet four inches (presumably sight measure).
The eyes are a darkish grey, the hair reddish, fair
to light brown.   The sleeved garment is grey, and
the head is surmounted by a square drapery of the
same colour.   Three parts of the background
consist of a column and dark brown wall, and to
the left is a landscape.   On the column hangs the
small shield—party per pale arg. and gu., a bend
counterchanged.   "The picture," continues Mr.
T. E. King, who courteously sent me these particu-
lars, " is clean and fresh.   There is a good deal of
character in the face, which is deeply lined, especially about the corners of the mouth."

This portrait, it will be seen, is based originally
upon the Occleve limning, or upon a copy of it,
while the seventeenth-century landscape background
and general Flemish manner betray it.   At the same
time, it resembles more closely the Seddon or
Fairfax Murray portrait than any other.   From
what we know of the custom of the time—and
confirmed in the belief by the nature of Evelyn's
own testimony—it is likely that the first Earl
Clarendon, desiring to have portraits of our poets,
etc., for his room, adopted the simple expedient of
having them painted for him, instructing the artist
to depend not entirely on his own inspiration, but
to go to such authority as he could find.

It will be noticed that the beads of the rosary are
red and black, but not in couples—they are arranged
alternately.   Thirty-one beads are visible; a cross

of gold hangs from a clasp of the same metal, and two other clasps at the sides break the series.

X. Another portrait contained in the Bodleian Library is here reproduced, more for completeness' sake than from the belief that any sort of historic interest belongs to it. This is the pastel portrait founded, very infelicitously, on the Occleve portrait. The evident attempt to beautify the face, to refine the somewhat aquiline nose of the original, to clear-cut its tip and idealise its nostril, to diminish the size of the ear while transferring it to a more appropriate place than that where Occleve put it, to raise the lips in a smile instead of depressing them as in the original, to curl the hair, and give a dashing twist to the moustache and a flow to the little beard, to accentuate the eyes (yet only succeeding in making them squint), and generally to smarten up the poet and show him as something of a dandy—robbing him at once of his dignity and of his simplicity of dress, and endowing him with em-broideries—this is the work of a fairly skilful but unsympathetic draughtsman, wholly ignorant of Chaucer's temperament, intellect, or personality. Yet the picture, modern as it appears, has been a good while in the Library, the records of which set forth that this portrait, "in crayons," was be-queathed by Dr. Richard Rawlinson in 1755. It is almost certainly an eighteenth century work.

We thus have ten principal portraits (but of very unequal interest and value) which are dealt with here, and these, for the sake of convenience, I re-enumerate :

PLATE X.

THE RAWLINSON PASTEL PORTRAIT. BODLEIAN LIBRARY, OXFORD.

 Adlard & Son, Imp.

1. Occleve, Harleian MS. 4866 . . .	British Museum .	. Half length.
2. Occleve, Royal MS. 17 D. vi . . .	British Museum .	. Full length.
3. Add. MS. 5141 . .	British Museum .	. Full length.
4. Lansdowne MS. 851 .	British Museum .	. Full length.
5. Sloane Collection .	National Portrait Gallery	Full length.
6. Bodleian . . .	Bodleian Library .	. Half length.
7. Seddon or Fairfax Murray . . .	Mr. Fairfax Murray .	. Half length.
8. Ellesmere MS. (Equestrian) . . .	Bridgewater House .	. Full length.
9. Clarendon . . .	Bothwell Castle .	. Half length.
10. Rawlinson pastel .	Bodleian Library .	. Quarter length.

If we would classify these portraits in any way, we should probably have to resort to the minor expedient of dividing them into the two variants in design—those which represent the poet as pointing forward with the index finger, as the two Occleve and the Ellesmere portraits, and those which show him fingering his penner, as in the Add. 5141 portrait, the Sloane, the Bodleian, and the Fairfax Murray portraits. It would be more satisfactory, perhaps, from the physiognomical point of view, could we separate those which attribute to Chaucer an aquiline nose from those which suggest a bulbous one. But seeing that there is only one portrait which we need freely accept, we can afford to regard the matter as of little relative importance, especially as all early portraitists have agreed in this—that the face as well as the bearing of Chaucer was full of quiet dignity and simple modesty, and that, whether painted work or engraving, nearly all representations succeed in impressing the spectator with these leading characteristics.   Much the same may be said of the frontispiece-portraits to the collected editions of his works.   It will be remembered that the 1532 edition and the two Stowe editions of 1542 and 1561 had no portrait; but Speght's folio of 1598 was so decorated, and nearly every important edition since that date has been provided with a plate better or less well executed.   When ill done they do not always claim the application of Macaulay's consolatory criticism, that the best portraits are those in which there is a slight mixture of caricature.   What would we not give to see the Master in just one photograph—the equivalent, or, at least, the substitute, of the mirror which Menzel declared to be better than a whole gallery of portraits?   That we have, as it is, so extensive a gallery of Chaucer portraits seems the more remarkable the more we study the history and practice of portrait-painting in Chaucer's time and onwards; and we can only conclude that the appreciation of his day was more acute than later on, when, if Dryden speak the truth, Cowley told the Earl of Leicester that Chaucer was a dry, old-fashioned wit, not worth reviving, and that he had no taste of him.*

There is no need to offer explanation for the interest which consideration of the features and the person of the poet must arouse in the mind of every one of his readers, or excuses for the enthusiasm with which an inquirer into the subject must prosecute his researches.   It is only the conviction that the Occleve portrait (Harleian 4866)

* Southey's 'Common-place Book,' vol. iv, p. 323.—M. H. S.

is the sole authentic picture that has prevented
Professor Skeat and Dr. Furnivall—the leaders of
modern Chaucerian students—from dealing with
the whole subject at length ; but a humbler inquirer
may well feel justified in going over the old ground,
seeking whether anything new may not be discovered by the re-turning of old stones, more particularly when he approaches the subject less from
the literary and historical side than from that of
art and physiognomy.

THE LIFE AND CHARACTERISTICS OF CHAUCER.

BY PERCY W. AMES, F.S.A.

[In certain of the quotations from Chaucer's poems contained in the following paper, the transliteration adopted by Mr. A. W. Ward has been employed, and for this, in addition to numerous suggestions afforded by the Professor's excellent essay on Chaucer, the writer desires to express his acknowledgments.]

MATTHEW ARNOLD used frequently to say that in literature we have present and prepared to form us, the best that has been thought and said in the world. Our business is obviously to get at this best and to know it well, but to do so we must have guidance and direction. The Council of our Society have instituted for this purpose these courses of afternoon lectures, in connection with which, however, some responsibility rests upon both lecturers and students in order that the maximum benefit and advantage may be derived from them. It is natural to expect from the lecturer, with regard to the subject he introduces, evidence of comprehensive and accurate knowledge, genuine sympathy and appreciation, and the power of so presenting his author as to give a real sense of his power and charm. On the other hand, it is not unreasonable to hope that the hearers will not rest content with the pastime of an hour's entertainment, but that they will store in their memories such facts and ideas as are really significant, and, above all, be induced to make a first-hand acquaintance with the literature introduced. Another but closely allied object of such lectures should also, if I may be allowed to say so, be constantly kept in mind, and that is, to so cultivate the general taste that the wide popularity enjoyed by sensational stories of small literary merit may be shared by works of distinction, that noble thought, whether in poetry or prose, should be appreciated as well as incident and adventure.

No apology is needed for introducing Chaucer to lovers of good literature, but I should like to mention a few reasons for specially commending his writings to your notice. In the first place we must observe he is our earliest great poet. Not great simply by comparison with his English predecessors and contemporaries, but great in many of his high gifts and qualities for all time. A second claim which the study of Chaucer has upon us is derived from the immeasurable service which he rendered to the English tongue. Coincident with the amalgamation into a homogeneous nation of the three Teutonic elements, Saxon, Dane, and Norman, and the aboriginal Celt, was the formation, out of the speech of these peoples, of the English language, copious and forcible, and adapted, as it has been said, to " all the highest purposes of the poet, the philosopher, and the orator." It was Chaucer, however, who proved and illustrated these capabilities, and by the magic of his touch raised a dialect into a language. Chaucer's work was a revelation of the unsuspected value and power of the English speech. People had been accustomed to look to the French for poems, stories, and light thought gracefully expressed. Chaucer showed them what their own tongue was capable of. The language could never be the same again after he lived, and wrote with an altogether new ease, grace, and fluid lucidity of style. A third reason for advocating the study of Chaucer is because he exhibits beyond any other writer in number and extent those qualities and characteristics which we regard as peculiarly and essentially English. I refer to his abundant good sense, his freedom from morbid mysticism and superstition, his hatred of cant, his penetrating observation, his vivid and accurate delineation of detail and graphic portraiture, his rich imagination, and irrepressible, genial and frolicsome humour. We regard and claim these qualities as English because they have been so abundantly exemplified in our writers since the time of Chaucer, but he was undoubtedly the first humorist in order of time, as well as our earliest great poet. A fourth reason has already been stated. Chaucer died in his house at Westminster, adjoining the White Rose tavern, and where now stands the gorgeous mausoleum of King Henry the Seventh, in the year 1400, and was the first poet to be buried in the South Transept of Westminster Abbey, and so gave the name of Poets' Corner to that spot so dear to the English literary student. This, then, is the five hundredth anniversary of the poet's death, and in accordance with the graceful custom of recent times we desire to commemorate the event by the study of his life, times, and works, and so to take a modest share in this year's commemoration.

As it is not advisable in a single lecture on Chaucer to dwell too long on the details of his life, I propose to give merely an outline, and to direct attention to such of his experiences as had an influence upon the development of his genius.

Geoffrey Chaucer was born about 1340, in a house near the foot of Dowgate Hill in Upper Thames Street. The spot is covered by a portion of Cannon Street Railway Station. His grandfather, Robert Chaucer, and his father, John, and his half-uncle, Thomas Heyroun, were all vintners or tavern-keepers, perhaps both, so Geoffrey was probably brought up in an atmosphere of gaiety and good cheer, and with unrivalled opportunities for seeing and hearing many varieties of men. We may certainly trace here the sources of his knowledge of the general style of the tavern-keeper of which he gives so admirable an example in Harry Bailly. From his early experiences Chaucer may also have acquired his disgust at drunkenness.

> " A lecherous thing is wine, and drunkenness
> Is full of striving and of wretchedness.
> O drunken man, disfigured is thy face,
> Sour is thy breath, foul art thou to embrace,
> And through thy drunken nose seemeth the soun'
> As though thou saidest aye " Sampsoun, Sampsoun,"
> And yet Got wot, Sampson drank never no wine.
> Thou fallest as it were a stikéd swine ;
> Thy tongue is lost and all thine honest cure ;
> For drunkenness is very sepulture
> Of man's wit and his discretion.
> In whom that drink hath domination
> He can no counsel keep, it is no drede."
>
> ('Pardoner's Tale.')

Chaucer's father was deputy to the king's butler, which may account for the fact that Geoffrey was introduced at an early age into the service of the royal family. At the age of seventeen he was a page in the household of Elizabeth, Countess of Ulster, wife of Lionel, Duke of Clarence, third son of Edward the Third. When he was nineteen years of age—that is in 1359—he first " bore arms." He accompanied the army to France, and was taken prisoner at Retiers, in Brittany, from which plight he was ransomed in March, 1360, the king contributing £16 towards the required amount. It is believed that in this year, at the age of twenty, he married Philippa de Roet, whose sister Katherine, the widow of Sir Hugh Swinford, later on became the third wife of John of Gaunt. The Thomas Chaucer who was a noticeable House of Commons man under the Lancastrians is supposed to have been the poet's eldest son, and born about 1362, but of this there is no satisfactory evidence. In 1365 his daughter Elizabeth was born, for whose novitiate, when she was sixteen, John of Gaunt paid £50 to the Abbey of Barking. In 1366 his father died, and in the same year we hear of Philippa Chaucer as one of the ladies of the queen's bedchamber. In 1367 a life-pension was granted to Chaucer by the King, when he is described as " our beloved yeoman " (*dilectus valettus noster*). In 1368 Chaucer's first patron, Prince Lionel, died, and his services were transferred to the next brother, John of Gaunt, whose first wife Blanche, Duchess of Lancaster, died in September, 1369, and for the first time Chaucer, who was of

the same age as his deceased mistress, viz. twenty-
nine, appears as a poet, although the 'Book of the
Duchess' was not probably his earliest writing.
From 1370 to 1386 Chaucer was frequently employed on diplomatic missions abroad. In December, 1372, he went on the King's service to
Italy, and visited Genoa, Pisa, and Florence. At
this time Bocaccio was living at Florence, and it is
quite possible that Chaucer met him, but though
he makes free use of Bocaccio's poems he never
mentions him by name. Petrarch was living near
Padua at the time of this visit, and from a passage
in the Clerk's prologue we may conclude Chaucer
certainly encountered him.

> "I will you tell a tale which that I
>   Learnëd at Padua of a worthy clerk,
>   As provëd by his wordës and his work.
>   He is now dead and nailëd in his chest,
>   I pray to God to give his soulë rest!
>   Francis Petrarck, the laureate poet,
>   Hightë this clerk, whose retoric sweet
>   Enlumined all Italy of poetry," etc.

This journey to Italy had a most important
effect upon Chaucer, for it brought him for the
first time directly under the influence of the Italian
renaissance, and his writings from this time forth
are of a wider range and of a higher poetic form.

On May 10th, 1374, Chaucer took a lease of a
house in Aldgate, where he resided for about ten
years, and, as Mr. Ward suggests, we can picture
him walking daily through London's narrow streets

with their gabled houses, to and from this home
and the Custom House on the river side. In the
same year he was granted by the King a pitcher of
wine daily, appointed Comptroller of the Customs
and Subsidy of wools, skins, and leather for the
port of London, and received a life-pension of £10
from John of Gaunt. In June, 1377, Edward the
Third died and was succeeded by his grandson; but
these events did not interfere with Chaucer's good
fortune, as he continued to be employed upon political missions. In 1378, on being again sent to
Italy, he appointed his friend John Gower, the
poet, as one of his agents to represent him during
his absence.

In 1385 we find Chaucer living in the country,
in all probability at Greenwich, where he had a
garden and a little arbour with a grassy couch,
which he describes. In September, 1390, he was
twice robbed, apparently on the same day, of the
King's money; the first time at Westminster of
£10, and again at Hatcham, while on his way home
to Greenwich, of £9 3s. 8d. He was excused from
repayment of these sums. Another event of this
year may have had some connection with his resi-
dence at the southern side. He was put on a
commission to repair the banks of the Thames between Woolwich and Greenwich.

In 1386 he was elected a knight of the shire of
Kent, but the Parliament of which he thus became
a member, after taking measures for opposing the
autocratical tendencies of Richard the Second, and
for securing financial reform, lent itself to the
schemes of the then head of the administration,

Thomas Duke of Gloucester, who, taking advantage of the absence in France of his brother and political rival, John of Gaunt, proceeded to replace certain holders of office by nominees of his own, and our friend Chaucer was one of the victims. In December of this year he lost both his appointments and was reduced to poverty, and ill-fortune pursued him almost to the end of his life. Although in 1390 he was appointed Clerk of the Works at St. George's Chapel at Windsor, and in 1394 received a grant of £20 a year for life, he nevertheless seems to have been in want of money, as he frequently applied for advanced payments. In September, 1399, Henry the Fourth, the son of his old patron, became King of England, and Chaucer addressed to him a complaint of his poverty, and the new monarch promptly doubled his pension.

I propose now to make an attempt to present the man himself, and to illustrate from his own inimitable utterances the several brilliant qualities of his most attractive personality.

When the student who is thoroughly familiar with the writings of Chaucer is asked to specify his different qualities, it is probable that he would mention first the gaiety and brightness, the vivacity and joyousness of his temperament and disposition. Chaucer had his troubles, some of them indeed of the saddest description. He had that bitter experience, for instance, of being suddenly reduced from affluence to poverty, and may have had this in his mind when he thus rendered Francesca's lines in the Inferno :

" (Nessun maggior dolore
 Che ricordarsi del tempo felice
 Nella miseria)."
" For, of Fortunës sharp adversité,
 The worstë kynde of infortúne is this,
 A man to have been in prosperité,
 And it remember, whanne it passëd is."

In 1387 he lost his wife, and a few years later death robbed the widower of his little son Lewis, for whom he had affectionately compiled in admirable prose the 'Treatise on the Astrolabe.' Chaucer therefore had his troubles; but, as Mr. Lecky says, "Happiness is a condition of Mind and not a disposition of circumstances." * It would be a serious mistake to suppose that Chaucer's gaiety arose from an inability to feel deeply, but he had not that over-refined conscience which indulges in excessive introspection, torturing self-analysis and self-reproach. He wasted no mental or moral energy on barren speculations, and to him might be applied what Locke sensibly said of himself, he was content to sit down in quiet ignorance of transcendental questions. Chaucer was our first eminent poet of Love, in which character he displays much of Shakespeare's exquisite naturalism. Although he gives many beautiful examples of the faithfulness of lovers under circumstances of trial and sorrow, yet for the most part it is the bright, the merry, the successful aspects of this many-sided passion on which he prefers to dwell. Chaucer's liveliness is amusingly shown in the midst of his most serious

* 'Map of Life.'

and pathetic descriptions. Usually it is the reader who becomes tired of prolonged narratives of sadness, but here the author frequently manifests an impatience and interrupts himself when the narrative is in danger of becoming too pitiable or diffuse. "Men," he says, "may overlade a ship or barge, and therefore I will skip at once to the effect, and let all the rest slip." He excuses himself from the task of describing all the details of a marriage feast by saying—

> "The fruit of every tale is for to say:
> They eat and drink, and dance and sing and play."

In 'Troilus and Cressida' he suddenly hurries on his narrative :

> "But flee we now prolixitee best is,
> For love of god, and lat us fastë go
> Right to the effect, with-outë talës mo."

Again :

> "He gan him recommande unto her grace ;
> To tell all how, it axeth muchel space."

And in another piece :

> "For now will I go streight to my matére."

In the 'Book of the Duchess,' written to commemorate the death of Blanche of Lancaster, the sad and inconsolable widower suddenly forgets apparently his ultra-melancholy and woebegone state, and gives a lively description of his lost love, which may serve as a portrait of a bright English girl of any age :

"I saw her dance so comelily,
Caról and sing so sweetëly,
And laugh and play so womanly,
And lookë so debónairly,
So goodly speak and so friendly,
That sure I trow that nevermore
Was seen so blissful a tresúre.
For every hair upon her head,
Sooth to say it was not red,
Nor yellow neither, nor brown it was,
Methought most likë gold it was.
And ah! what eyes my lady had,
Debónair, goodë, glad and sad,
Simple, of good size, not too wide
Therto her look was not aside
Nor overthwart, but set so well
It drew and took up every del
All that on her gan beholde."

The poet further tells us that her kind and gentle glances made fools think some special favour was intended, but that was their delusion, for—

"It was no counterfeited thing,
It was her ownë pure looking."

Another characteristic equally ubiquitous is Chaucer's *humour*. He had the keenest sense of the ludicrous, the incongruous, and the comical in life and manners and circumstance. Professor Ward suggests that the truest explanation of why Chaucer is so extremely diverting is that he was so extremely diverted himself. One of the literary products of modern times which we could very well do without is the book written to order. If a man

in temporary good health and spirits writes a
humorous book, the demands of the market require
that he should write another. Nothing is more
pitiable in its utter melancholy than such laborious
attempts to be funny. In refreshing contrast with
these cemeteries of mirth and jollity, is the constant
flow of genuine and effortless humour which is so
perfectly natural to Chaucer. As Mr. Ward says,
" His humour has many varieties, ranging from the
refined and half-melancholy irony of the ' House of
Fame,' to the ready wit of the sagacious uncle of
Cressid, the burlesque fun of the inimitable ' Nun's
Priest's Tale,' and the very gross salt of the Reeve
and the Miller." Chaucer was gifted with the
power of ridiculing the follies and hypocrisies of
his day equally with any humorist who has followed
him, but his satire is never fierce or bitter—like
Swift's, for instance. His severest satire perhaps
is to be found in the self-description he puts in the
mouth of the Pardoner, whose wallet was brimful
of pardons come from Rome all hot. The best way
to enjoy Chaucer is to try to read him in the same
merry, jovial, and light-hearted spirit in which he
wrote. Most of Chaucer's humour is perfectly
innocent harmless fun, but far too frequently in
his Tales he descends to downright coarseness, and
this is all the more reprehensible for the raciness
and gusto which he throws into his style; but how
amusingly he answers the charge of impropriety
that was brought against him in his own day. He
declares that he must tell stories in character, and
coolly requests any person who may find anything
in one of his tales objectionable to turn to another :

"For he shall find enough, both great and small,
Of storial thing that toucheth gentleness,
Likewise morality and holiness;
Blame ye not me, if ye should choose amiss."

Most of the descriptions of the Canterbury
Pilgrims have a touch of humour in them. How
ridiculous and yet effective is his observation of a
very thin man that he looked *hollow*, and that his
horse was like a *rake;* or of the strong bony miller
that there was no door that he could not break at
a running with his head. In Chaucer's time there
appear to have been medical practitioners who were
bitten with worldly ambition and love of wealth,
and he slyly alludes to this in his description of the
Doctour of Phisyk—

"In scarlet and in blue he clad was al,
Lyned with taffata and with sendal;
And yet he was but easy in dispence;
He keptë that he won in pestilence;
For gold in phisik is a cordial,
Therefore he lovede gold in special."

Harry Bailly, who acts as so effective a chorus to
the pilgrims, and was a master of japes and chaff
and banter, occasionally drew upon himself the
same kind of treatment. The Pardoner, after in-
viting the pilgrims to purchase his relics, suggests

"That our host here shall begin,
For he is most envelopéd in sin."

When the gallant Troilus is first smitten so deeply
with love for Cressid, and is in great despondency,
his friend Pandarus rallies him by pretending that

fear of the Greeks has made him bewail his sins, and says—

> " God save 'em that besiegéd have our town,
>   And so can lay our jollity on press
>   And bring our lusty folk to holiness !"

Although Chaucer has been described as chiefly a comic poet, yet very few writers have equalled him, and none have surpassed him, in pathos. This is well illustrated in the description of Arcite's deathbed in the ' Knight's Tale ;' also in the piteous lament of Constance in the tale of the ' Man of Law :'

> " Her little child lay weeping on her arm,
>   And kneeling, piteously to him she said,
>   ' Peace, little son, I will do thee no harm.'
>   With that her kerchief of her head she breyde
>   And over his little eyen she it laid ;
>   And in her arm she lulleth it full faste,
>   And into heaven her eyen up she cast.
>
> Moder, quod she, and mayde bright Marye,
>   Sooth is that through woman's incitement
>   Mankind was lorn and condemned to dye,
>   For which thy child was on a croys y-rent ;
>   Thy blissful eyen saw all his torment ;
>   Then is there no comparison between
>   Thy wo and any wo man may sustene.
>
> Thou saw thy child y-slayn before thine eyen,
>   And yet now liveth my little child parfay.
>   Now, lady bright, to whom all woful cryen,
>   Thou glorie of womanhood, thou faire may,
>   Thou haven of refuge, bright star of day,
>   Rewe on my child, that of thy gentleness
>   Rewest on every rewful in distress !

O little child, alas! what is thy guilt,
That never wroughtest sin as yet, pardee,
Why will thy harde father have thee spilt?"

and so on.

Also Anelida's letter to her false lover, and
Grisilde, although not unaptly termed a martyr to
unreason, certainly makes the 'Clerk's Tale' one
of the most pitiful and pathetic in the language.

Not the least interesting characteristic of Chaucer
was his genuine love of nature. Spring-time was
his favourite season, when the trees and meadows
and hedgerows were dressed in their freshest,
brightest colours. From several hints he gives us
we know that he was a devoted book-lover, and
used to spend his evenings reading as " still as any
stone," but at the early signs of returning summer
he threw aside his books, and found solace and
delight in the unfolding of the flowers and the
songs of the birds. In the prologue to the 'Legend
of Good Women,' he says :

" And as for me, though that I can but lyte
On bookës for to read I me delyte,
And to em give I faith and ful credence,
And in my herte have hem in reverence
So hertely, that there is gamë none
That from my bokës maketh me begone.
But hit be seldom, on the holyday ;
Save, certeynly, when that the month of May
Is come, and that I here the foulës singe,
And that the flourës ginnen for to springe,
Farwel my book and my devocion."

In his address to the daisy he tells us how in May-
time he was always up—

> " And walking in the mead
> To see this flow'r against the sunnë spread,
> When it upriseth early by the morrow,
> That blissful sight softeneth all my sorrow."

Again—

> " The busy lark, messenger of day,
> Saluteth in her song the morrow gray;
> And fiery Phœbus riseth up so bright,
> That all the orient laugheth with the light;
> And with his stremës dryeth in the greves
> The silver dropës hanging on the leves."

Chaucer's numerous references to nature's charms and beauties convince the reader that it was not a mere conformity with the conventional May morning exaudia of the French poets, but a genuine sympathy and true admiration, and they illustrate also his close and accurate observation. Chaucer effectively employs this power by way of illustration. For instance, the desolate condition of the deserted Troilus is thus described :

> " And as in winter, levës been bireft
> Each after other till the tree be bare,
> So that ther nis but bark and branch y-left,
> Lyeth Troilus, bireft of each wel-fare."

His powers of description were of an extremely high order. On the sublime side few scenes in literature surpass his vision of the Temple of Mars, while one of the most beautiful is the picture of Emelye in the garden; both in the ' Knight's Tale.'

Chaucer's philosophy of life may be expressed in the word *toleration*. He had little sympathy with enthusiasm, and disliked extremes. He sympathised with Wiclifism only so far as it attempted to relieve the simple fundamental ethics of Christianity from the artificial and superstitious fabric of observances with which they had been overlaid. When Lollardry became identified with political reform, Chaucer, like his patron and brother-in-law, John of Gaunt, became estranged from it. We must remember that all his life he had been closely connected with the royal family. He was a courtier, a civil servant, and a diplomatist, and we need not therefore be surprised that he did not identify himself with the sadly unsuccessful attempts at social and political reform of his time. We know, however, that he hated injustice and oppression as much as he despised cant and hypocrisy. In the following passage from the ' Parson's Tale,' he nobly advocates the cause of the poor :

"Think also that of the same seed of which churls spring, of the same seed spring lords; as well may the churl be saved as the lord. Wherefore I counsel thee do just so with thy churl as thou wouldest thy lord did with thee if thou wert in his plight. . . . I counsel thee certainly, thou lord, that thou work in such wise with thy churls that they rather love thee than dread thee. I know well where there is degree above degree it is reasonable that men should do their duty where it is due; but of a certainty extortions, and despite of our underlings, are damnable."

On the whole, moderation in view and judgment was characteristic of Chaucer. One illustration out of many may be selected. These words he puts into the mouth of Cressid :

"In everything I woot ther lyth mesúre,
 For though a man forbede dronkenesse,
He nought for-bet that every créature,
 Be drinkeless for alwey, as I guess."

That Chaucer deeply felt the beauty of genuine unaffected piety is amply proved in his description of the Parson in the famous 'Prologue,' one of the noblest pictures in all literature:

"A good man was there of religion
And was a poorë Parson of a town
But rich he was of holy thought and work.
He was also a learnèd man, a clerk
That Christës Gospel truly woulde preach;
And his parishioners devoutly teach.
Benign he was and wondrous diligent,
And in adversity full patient.
And such he was y-provèd ofte sithes.
Full loth he was to curse men for his tithes;
But rather would he givë, without doubt,
Unto his poor parishioners about
Of his off'ríng and eke of his substánce,
He could in little wealth have súffisance.
Wide was his parish, houses far asunder,
Yet failed he not for either rain or thunder
In sickness nor mischance to visit all
The furthest in his parish, great and small,
Upon his feet, and in his hand a staff.
This noble ensample to his sheep he gave,
That first he wrought, and afterwards he taught
Out of the Gospel he those wordës caught,
And this figúre he added eke thereto,
That "if gold rustë, what shall iron do?"
For if a priest be foul, on whom we trust,
No wonder is it if a layman rust;
And shame it is, if that a priest take keep,
A foul shepherd to see and a clean sheep;

Well ought a priest ensample for to give
By his cleanness, how that his sheep should live.
He put not out his benefice on hire,
And left his sheep encumbered in the mire,
And ran to London unto Sainté Paul's,
To seek himself a chantery for souls,
Or maintenance with a brotherhood to hold,
But dwelt at home, and kepté well his fold,
So that the wolf ne'er made it to miscarry ;
He was a shepherd and no mercenary.
And though he holy were, and virtuous,
He was to sinful man not déspitous,
And of his speech not difficult nor digne,
But in his teaching díscreet and benign.
For to draw folk to heaven by fairnéss,
By good ensample, this was his business ;
But were there any person obstinate,
What so he were, of high or low estate,
Him would he sharply snub at once.   Than this
A better priest, I trow, there nowhere is.
He waited for no pomp and reverence,
Nor made himself a spicéd consciénce ;
But Christés lore and His Apostles' twelve
He taught, but first he followed it himself."

Of almost equal beauty is Chaucer's discourse
on bearing and forbearing in friendship, which Mr.
Ward truly describes as combining a ripe wisdom
with the ethics of true gentleness. This is from
the ' Franklin's Tale : '

"For one thing sirës, safely dare I say,
That friends the one the other must obey,
If they will longë holdë company.
Love will not be constrain'd by mastery.
When mastery comes, the god of love anon
Beateth his wings—and farewell he is gone.

Love is a thing as any spirit free.
Women desire, by nature, liberty,
And not to be constrainèd as a thrall,
And so do men, if I the truth say shall.
Look, who that is most patient in love,
He is at his advantage all above.
A virtue high is patience certain,
Because it vanquisheth, as clerks explain,
Things to which rigour never could attain.
For every word men should not chide and plain ;
Learn ye to suffer, or else, so may I go,
Ye shall it learn, whether ye will or no.
For in this world certain no wight there is
Who neither doth nor saith some time amiss.
Sickness, or ire, or constellation,
Wine, woe, or changing of complexion,
Causeth full oft to do amiss or speak.
For every wrong men may not vengeance wreak.
After a time there must be temperance
With every wight that knows self-governance."

From the examples of Chaucer's versification
already given to illustrate various points, the melody
of his word-music must have been noticed, but I
am tempted to make one or two quotations to
demonstrate this poetic charm. Many lines might
be selected to prove the perfection of Chaucer in
this respect. "What is the nature of the art,"
asks Mr. Ward, "at whose bidding ten mono-
syllables arrange themselves into a line of the
exquisite cadence of the following ?

"'And she was fair, as is the rose in May.'"

And again :

"For pity runneth soon in gentle heart."

And the lament of Medea when deserted by Jason has its own melancholy charm:

" Why likéd thee my yellow hair to see
  More than the boundës of mine honesty?
  Why likéd me thy youth and thy fairnéss
  And of thy tongue the infinite graciousness?
  O, had'st thou in thy conquest dead y-bee
  Full muckle untruth had there died with thee."

There is quite a divine beauty in Chaucer's religious poems. I can only venture to quote one, the hymn to the Virgin in the prologue to the ' Prioress's Tale: '

" O mother maid! O maiden mother free!
  O bush unburnt, burning in Moses' sight,
  That didst draw down from the Deity,
  Through thine humblesse, the soul that in th' alighte,
  Of whose virtue, when he thine herte lighte,
  Conceivéd was the father's sapience,
  Help me to tell it in thy reverence!

" Lady! thy bounty, thy magnificence,
  Thy virtue and thy great humility
  There may no tongue express in no science;
  For sometime, lady, ere men pray to thee
  Thou goest before of thy benignity
  And gettest us the light through thy preyere
  To guide us unto thy son so dear.

" My cunning is so weak, O blissful queen,
  For to declare thy great worthiness,
  That I may not the weight of it sustain
  But as a child of twelve months old or less,
  That scarcely can a word express,
  Right so fare I, and therefore I you pray
  To guide my song that I shall of you say."

Chaucer's extraordinary powers of observation are in no direction more strikingly exhibited than in his references to and descriptions of women. So freely scattered about his writings are facetious remarks concerning women and their favourite foibles that the poet has brought upon himself the charge that he was seriously lacking in respect and true chivalry. Yet few poets have given so many and such striking examples of the gentleness and fidelity of women as Chaucer. The clerk of Oxford says :

> " Men speak of Job, most for his humbleness,
> As clerkës, when they list, may well indite,
> Of men in special; but in truthfulness,
> Though praise by clerks of women be but slight,
> No man in humbleness can him acquit
> As women can, nor can be half so true
> As women are, unless all things be new."

The highest and at the same time the most essential and characteristic quality of Chaucer's genius is his dramatic power. The drama as a literary form did not then exist, or we can easily suppose Chaucer would have found in it his most natural and congenial mode of expression. As it was he had to adopt the narrative form, but the dramatic power is plainly there. This is shown in the individualism of his characters generally. Cressid, for example, is as real and natural as any human being ever portrayed in literature. The dramatic quality, however, is most strikingly exhibited in the ' Canterbury Pilgrims.' These are not only realistic and vivid, but each is a type of a class, as definite as the characters in

Shakespeare. Then, again, they are made to un-
fold and reveal themselves by a threefold process.
First, they are described with extraordinary vigour
and animation in the general ' Prologue.' Secondly,
they partly describe themselves in their own pro-
logues. Thirdly, the leading feature of their
character is illustrated by the tales which they tell.

The Wife of Bath, for example, is graphically
portrayed in the ' Prologue.' She was a travelling
dealer in cloth ; she had a bold face, fair and red ;
she had likewise red stockings, and her shoes were
soft, supple, and new, and fitted well; the kerchiefs
on her head were of the finest quality, and on Sun-
days weighed as much as ten pounds ; she had been
married five times ; there was not a woman in Bath
who dared to pass in front of her in church, but if
one did so by chance she was very wroth and out
of all charity.

> " Upon an ambler easily she sat,
> Y-wimpled well, and on her head a hat,
> As broad as is a buckler or a targe."

Her teeth were not close together, but had little
spaces between them, and she calls attention herself
to this peculiarity, remarking that it is very becoming. Her prologue, which is the most plain-spoken
address ever delivered by a woman, is based with
comical audacity on the ' Treatise on Perpetual
Virginity,' by St. Jerome. In this " long preamble
to a tale," as the Frere called it, we perceive not
only " the ceaseless chatter of an indomitable
tongue," but obtain a fuller and more vivid representation of her individuality. In it she makes an

effective reference to the ancient custom, still preserved, of giving a flitch of bacon to the happiest
married couple. She boasts of the life she led each
of her husbands by her chiding tongue, and says :

> "The bacon was not fetched for them I trow,
> That some men have in Essex at Dunmow."

She is altogether an alarming person, and one may
be excused for feeling glad she is dead. On the
one hand she said that women are best won by
flattery and fine presents; that they tell untruths
and swear to them with twice the boldness of men.

> "For half so boldely can ther no man,
> Swere and lyen as a womman can."

On the other she declares :

> "By God, if women had but written stories,
> As clerkës have within their oratóries,
> They would have writ of men more wickednéss
> Than all the race of Adam may redress."

Finally her tale illustrates still further her leading
trait, for she there maintains that what women most
desire is sovereignty over their husbands.

In the same way the chivalrous character of the
knight, old-fashioned even then, is unfolded, and
he is similarly fitted with a tale which gives point
to his own rather Quixotic peculiarities. So with
the Clerk, the Second Nun, the gentle Prioress,
as well as with the grosser characters. In all
these Chaucer reveals a delicate, penetrating, and
consummate insight, and in the framework and
entire treatment of the whole, art, poetry, and
genius are abundantly manifest.

The suggestion has been made that Chaucer derived the idea of the 'Canterbury Tales' from
Boccaccio; but this is unnecessary, as the method of
linking tales together is a very ancient device. If,
however, we compare Chaucer's plan with the
'Decamerone,' we perceive at once its immense
superiority. Boccaccio's characters were ladies and
gentlemen, all of the same class, who relieved the
tedium of a prolonged stay at a country house
during the plague by telling miscellaneous stories.
Chaucer's plan allowed quite naturally of a great
variety of typical characters being brought together. And the journey was an admirable device
for bringing out the peculiarities of the travellers.

Chaucer then was prolific in types of character and
aspects of life; lucid, graceful, easy and unre-
strained in style. For the appreciation of some
forms of literary art, more especially those in
which order and proportion are the chief characteristics, a little guidance seems necessary, and so
our admiration is not quite real and spontaneous;
but Chaucer, spirited, original, and joyous, at once
captivates and charms us, and it is only after our
first surprise that we begin to realise his value and
apportion him his place among the poets. Although,
like all true poets, Chaucer must have possessed a
range of sensibility far overlapping the ordinary
gamut, and a degree of intensity of feeling far trans-
cending the capacity of duller natures—for the soul
of the poet responds to harmonious undulations and
ecstatic visions which others do not perceive, and
experiences vivid emotions of misery or delight,
unsuspected perhaps by those nearest to him,—yet

Chaucer's mind, highly and delicately organised as it probably was, remained at all times eminently sane; he was free from that not uncommon accompaniment of genius, viz. an uncontrollable irregularity of thought and expression.

In order to obtain a clear, reliable, and useful idea of a poet it is necessary to note his limitations and deficiencies as well as his undoubted excellences, and by the aid of comparison we may arrive at a just estimate of the qualities and characteristics, inclusive and exclusive, of Chaucer's genius. Most students are agreed in the opinion that he did not possess much strength of genuine passion, and that he was deficient in grandeur, idealism, and in lofty and sustained imagination. True nobility of style is only rarely met with in Chaucer's works. He resembled Boccaccio in his insensibility to the emotions of patriotism, and he was not over-burdened with a sense of the deep mystery of life. As Hallam shrewdly says, "it is chiefly as a comic poet, and a minute observer of manners and circumstances, that he excels. In serious and moral poetry he is frequently languid and diffuse; but he springs like Antæus from the earth when his subject changes to coarse satire or merry narrative." It cannot be said of Chaucer, as it has so justly been said of Wordsworth, that he taught men reverence, and revealed the hidden beauties of existence; still less is the remark applicable to him that "he uttered nothing base." We do not get from him such inspiration as from Coleridge, nor has he the power of Dante, Milton, or even Byron, of lifting the mind on the wings of imagination far away from earth, until it is lost in the contemplation of infinity, eternity, and omnipotence. Chaucer was of the earth earthy, but there was nothing sordid, mawkish, or unwholesome in his view of life and in his love of it; and his sunny nature was incapable of the "profound malignity of Dante's pietism," which makes that noble poet such an anomaly.

When we have read and enjoyed a great author, we are led inevitably to indulge in comparison, and to consider his fitting place in the temple of taste erected in that kingdom of the beautiful wherein we imagine all those gracious beings to be who have illumined the world by the light of genius. Chaucer's high reputation and exalted position in English literature (for it is only disputed as to whether he should occupy the second or third place after Shakespeare) are chiefly due to his greatest achievement, the 'Prologue' to the 'Canterbury Tales.' This rich piece of descriptive writing is not only one of England's glories, as being unique in all literature, but it is of the highest value historically, as furnishing the fullest, most accurate and vivid pictures of the various special and particular types of human society in the later Middle Ages. Dryden said, " I see all the pilgrims in the ' Canterbury Tales,' their humours, their features, and the very dress as distinctly as if I had supped with them at the Tabard in Southwark. Some of his persons are vicious and some virtuous, some are unlearned and some are learned. Even the ribaldry of the low characters is different—the Reeve, the Miller, and the Cook are several men, and distinguished from each other as much as the mincing

12

Lady Prioress and the broad-speaking, gap-toothed Wife of Bath." Ten Brink says, "We receive such an exact idea of the men he is describing that we can almost see them bodily before us. The poet's intuition and powers of observation are quite as wonderful as the art by which he lets his characters grow gradually before our eyes." And James Russell Lowell said, "One of the world's three or four great story-tellers, he was also one of the best versifiers that ever made English trip and sing with a gaiety that seems careless, but where every foot beats time to the time of the thought."

Even if any are disposed to dispute the high position which we incline to give to Chaucer, all must agree with Matthew Arnold's assertion, "With him is born our real poetry." However interesting to us, as English students, may be the literary productions of our country in early times, when the minstrel poets sang their alliterative songs of famous deeds, or chanted in equally pompous measure the peaceful teachings of Christianity, yet down to Chaucer's time our literature remained in an infantile state, crude and imperfect, exhibiting nothing beyond the rough draft of genuine poetry. We had indeed other writers of genius who struggled with the belated language in their efforts to give expression to their feelings, but the first great master was Chaucer, who came "like a bright morning in an early spring." It was his buoyant soul that developed, expanded, and enriched our literature, so that henceforth the English race also has the "air of nobility stamped upon its brow," for it has been touched with the golden

wand of genius, and has proved its royal kinship
with the nations possessed of the gift of song,
the sense of harmonious beauty, and the divine
power of enshrining their thought in forms of
incomparable grace.

PRINTED BY ADLARD AND SON, BARTHOLOMEW CLOSE, E.C.